Better Homes and Gardens®

HOMETOWN POTLUCK ★ FAVORITES

Serving sizes for all occasions, LARGE or SMALL

p. 9

p. 48

p. 146

p. 178

p. 170

Better Homes and Gardens® Books
Des Moines, Iowa

Better Homes and Gardens® Books
An imprint of Meredith® Books

HOMETOWN POTLUCK FAVORITES

Editor: Kristi M. Fuller
Senior Associate Design Director: John Eric Seid
Copy Chief: Terri Fredrickson
Copy and Production Editor: Victoria Forlini
Editorial Operations Manager: Karen Schirm
Managers, Book Production: Pam Kvitne, Marjorie J. Schenkelberg
Contributing Copy Editor: Maria Duryée
Contributing Proofreaders: Gretchen Kauffman, Susie Kling, Elise Marton
Indexer: Martha Fifield
Electronic Production Coordinator: Paula Forest
Editorial and Design Assistants: Karen McFadden, Mary Lee Gavin
Test Kitchen Director: Lynn Blanchard
Test Kitchen Product Supervisor: Marilyn Cornelius, Jennifer Kalinowski

Meredith® Books
Publisher and Editor in Chief: James D. Blume
Design Director: Matt Strelecki
Managing Editor: Gregory H. Kayko
Executive Editor, Food and Crafts: Jennifer Dorland Darling

Director, Operations: George A. Susral
Director, Production: Douglas M. Johnston

Vice President and General Manager: Douglas J. Guendel

***Better Homes and Gardens*® Magazine**
Editor in Chief: Karol DeWulf Nickell
Deputy Editor, Food and Entertaining: Nancy Hopkins

Meredith Publishing Group
President, Publishing Group: Stephen M. Lacy
Vice President-Publishing Director: Bob Mate

Meredith Corporation
Chairman and Chief Executive Officer: William T. Kerr

Chairman of the Executive Committee: E. T. Meredith III

All of us at Better Homes and Gardens® Books are dedicated to providing
you with the information and ideas you need to create delicious foods.
We welcome your comments and suggestions. Write to us at: Better Homes
and Gardens Books, Cookbook Editorial Department, 1716 Locust St.,
Des Moines, IA 50309-3023.

If you would like to purchase any of our cooking, crafts, gardening, home
improvement, or home decorating and design books, check wherever quality
books are sold. Or visit us at: bhgbooks.com

Pictured on front cover: Shepherd's Pie (see recipe, page 94)

Our Better Homes and Gardens® Test Kitchen seal assures you that every recipe in *Hometown Potluck Favorites* has been tested in the Better Homes and Gardens® Test Kitchen. This means that each recipe is practical and reliable, and meets our high standards of taste appeal. We guarantee your satisfaction with this book for as long as you own it.

TABLE OF CONTENTS

CHAPTER 1

BOASTFUL BEGINNINGS

p. 9 p. 12

p. 16 p. 24

p. 26 p. 28

FOR MORE RECIPES

Visit our Recipe Center at www.bhg.com/bkrecipe

**Queso Fondue
with Corn Bread Dippers, p.14**

Chunky Guacamole

Lime juice adds the zing to this version of guacamole—a party favorite any time of year.

PREP: 20 minutes CHILL: 1 hour

16 SERVINGS	INGREDIENTS	8 SERVINGS
2 medium	plum tomato(es), seeded and cut up	1 medium
2	fresh jalapeño chile pepper(s), seeded and chopped	1
1/4 cup	coarsely chopped red onion	2 Tbsp.
2 Tbsp.	lime juice	1 Tbsp.
1 Tbsp.	olive oil	1 1/2 tsp.
1/4 tsp.	salt	1/8 tsp.
1/8 tsp.	black pepper	Dash
2 cloves	garlic, halved	1 clove
2	ripe avocado(s), halved, seeded, peeled, and cut up	1
1/2 cup	snipped fresh cilantro	1/4 cup
	Tortilla chips	

1 In a food processor bowl combine tomatoes, red onion, lime juice, olive oil, salt, pepper, and garlic. Cover and process until mixture is coarsely chopped. Add avocados. Cover and process just until mixture is chopped. Transfer to a serving bowl; cover surface with plastic wrap. Chill for up to 1 hour. Serve with chips. Makes 2 cups for 16 servings and 1 cup for 8 servings.

To tote: Transport in an insulated container with ice packs. Place chips in an airtight bag or container.

NUTRITION FACTS PER SERVING: 48 cal., 5 g total fat (1 g sat. fat), 0 mg chol., 40 mg sodium, 2 g carbo., 1 g fiber, 1 g pro.
DAILY VALUES: 4% vit. A, 7% vit. C, 2% iron

Crab-Caper Dip

This elegant dip is perfect for special occasions. A hollowed-out round bread loaf creates an edible serving container.

1 Cut the top off the bread loaf and hollow out the inside. Place top and hollow bread loaf in an airtight container. Set aside.

2 In a medium saucepan cook onions, covered, in a small amount of boiling water for 5 minutes; drain well. In a large bowl stir together the cooked onions, mayonnaise dressing, Swiss cheese, crabmeat, and capers.

3 Spoon crab mixture into a 1¹/₂-quart casserole. Bake, covered, in a 350° oven about 55 minutes or until heated through. Serve with vegetable dippers.

*For 8 servings: Omit the loaf of bread; substitute sliced party bread. Prepare dip using method above, except cook onion in a small saucepan. Stir dip together in a small bowl; transfer dip to a 1¹/₂-cup casserole or ramekin. Bake, covered, in a 350° oven about 30 minutes or until heated through.

To tote: Transport dip in an insulated carrier. Transport bread loaf in an airtight container. To serve, spoon dip into hollowed-out bread loaf.

**NOTE: Reduced-fat cheese is preferable to regular-fat Swiss in this recipe because the reduced-fat cheese doesn't break down as easily during the long baking time required.

NUTRITION FACTS PER SERVING: 65 cal., 4 g total fat (1 g sat. fat), 10 mg chol., 132 mg sodium, 4 g carbo., 1 g fiber, 3 g pro.
DAILY VALUES: 54% vit. A, 33% vit. C, 7% calcium, 1% iron

PREP: 25 minutes
BAKE: 55 minutes OVEN: 350°F

40 SERVINGS — INGREDIENTS — 8 SERVINGS

40 SERVINGS	INGREDIENTS	8 SERVINGS
1 8- to 10-in.	round bread loaf, unsliced	omit*
2 cups	chopped onions	¹/₂ cup
2 cups	light mayonnaise dressing	¹/₂ cup
8 oz. (2 cups)	sliced reduced-fat Swiss cheese, finely chopped**	2 oz. (¹/₂ cup)
1 cup	cooked lump crabmeat, drained and flaked OR	¹/₄ cup
1 6-oz. can	crabmeat, drained and flaked	¹/₄ 6-oz. can
¹/₂ cup	capers, drained	1 Tbsp.
	Assorted vegetable dippers	

Strawberry Dip

Leftovers will store for up to a week in the refrigerator. Simply stir before serving to fluff up the dip.

1 Place cream cheese in a medium mixing bowl. Add marshmallow creme and beat with an electric mixer on low to medium speed until smooth. Transfer to a serving bowl. Use as a dip for strawberries. If desired, serve nuts, coconut, and/or chocolate for rolling dipped strawberries in. Makes 1½ cups for 24 servings and ¾ cup for 12 servings.

To tote: Cover tightly. Place strawberries in an airtight bag or container. Transport dip, strawberries, and, if desired, accompaniments in an insulated cooler with ice packs.

NUTRITION FACTS PER SERVING: 81 cal., 4 g total fat (2 g sat. fat), 10 mg chol., 33 mg sodium, 12 g carbo., 2 g fiber, 1 g pro.
DAILY VALUES: 3% vit. A, 68% vit. C, 2% calcium, 2% iron

START TO FINISH: 10 minutes

INGREDIENTS

24 SERVINGS		12 SERVINGS
1 8-oz. pkg.	cream cheese, softened	½ 8-oz. pkg.
1 7-oz. jar	marshmallow creme	½ 7-oz. jar (1 cup)
	Whole strawberries	
	Finely chopped nuts, toasted coconut, and/or shaved chocolate or miniature semisweet chocolate pieces (optional)	

Fresh Summer Salsa

Fresh salsa made from your own garden vegetables surpasses any store-bought version.

PREP: 40 minutes
STAND: 30 minutes   CHILL: 1 to 24 hours

INGREDIENTS

12 SERVINGS		6 SERVINGS
¹/₄ cup	finely chopped red onion	2 Tbsp.
¹/₄ cup	ice water	2 Tbsp.
2 Tbsp.	white wine vinegar	1 Tbsp.
4	tomatillos, husked, rinsed, and finely chopped	2
³/₄ cup	finely chopped yellow cherry tomatoes	¹/₃ cup
²/₃ cup (2)	finely chopped plum tomato(es)	¹/₃ cup (1)
1¹/₂ tsp.	snipped fresh cilantro	1 tsp.
1 medium	fresh serrano chile pepper, seeded and finely chopped	1 small
1 tsp.	lime juice	¹/₂ tsp.
	Salt and black pepper	
	Tortilla chips	

1 In a bowl combine onion, ice water, and vinegar; let stand for 30 minutes. Drain onion mixture; stir in tomatillos, cherry tomatoes, plum tomatoes, cilantro, serrano pepper, and lime juice. Season to taste with salt and black pepper. Cover and chill for 1 to 24 hours. Serve salsa with tortilla chips.

To tote: Transport in an insulated cooler with ice packs. Pack chips in an airtight bag or container.

NUTRITION FACTS PER SERVING: 79 cal., 4 g total fat (1 g sat. fat), 0 mg chol., 78 mg sodium, 11 g carbo., 1 g fiber, 1 g pro.
DAILY VALUES: 2% vit. A, 8% vit. C, 2% calcium, 2% iron

Beer Cheese Spread

Ten minutes. That's all you need to make this stir-together appetizer spread. Don't let the insignificant amount of time you spend making it fool you. It tastes great!

1 Let the cheddar cheese stand at room temperature for 30 minutes.

2 In a medium bowl combine cheese, beer, tomato paste, Worcestershire sauce, and garlic powder. Beat with an electric mixer on medium speed until combined. Cover and chill for 2 to 24 hours. Serve with pita chips.

Test Kitchen Tip: To make toasted pita chips, halve 4 pita bread rounds crosswise; cut each half into six wedges. Place on a baking sheet. Toast in a 350°F oven for 5 to 10 minutes or until wedges are crisp. Makes 48 chips.

To tote: Transport spread in an insulated cooler with ice packs. Pack chips or crackers in an airtight bag or container.

NUTRITION FACTS PER SERVING: 137 cal., 7 g total fat (4 g sat. fat), 20 mg chol., 266 mg sodium, 13 g carbo., 1 g fiber, 7 g pro.
DAILY VALUES: 6% vit. A, 3% vit. C, 16% calcium, 4% iron

PREP: 10 minutes STAND: 30 minutes
CHILL: 2 to 24 hours

INGREDIENTS

12 SERVINGS		6 SERVINGS
2 cups	finely shredded cheddar cheese	1 cup
1/4 cup	beer	2 Tbsp.
3 Tbsp.	tomato paste	4 1/2 tsp.
2 tsp.	Worcestershire sauce	1 tsp.
1/4 tsp.	garlic powder	1/8 tsp.

Toasted pita chips,
assorted crackers, and/or
tortilla chips

Dilled Hummus with Vegetables

Plan on about one cup of fresh vegetables per serving for this delicious Middle Eastern bean dip.

10 SERVINGS — INGREDIENTS — **5 SERVINGS**

10 SERVINGS	INGREDIENTS	5 SERVINGS
2 15-oz. cans	garbanzo beans (chickpeas), rinsed and drained	1 15-oz. can
1/2 cup	tahini (sesame paste)	1/4 cup
1/3 cup	lemon juice	3 Tbsp.
2 Tbsp.	olive oil or cooking oil	1 Tbsp.
4 tsp.	snipped fresh dill OR	2 tsp.
1 tsp.	dried dill	1/2 tsp.
1/2 tsp.	salt	1/4 tsp.
1/8 tsp.	ground red pepper	Dash
4 cloves	garlic, minced	2 cloves
	Assorted vegetable dippers (such as broccoli florets, carrot sticks, and yellow sweet pepper strips)	

1 In a blender container or food processor bowl combine garbanzo beans, tahini, lemon juice, oil, dill, salt, red pepper, and garlic. Cover and blend or process until mixture is smooth, stopping and scraping sides as necessary. Cover and chill for up to 3 days. Stir hummus before serving. Serve with assorted vegetables.

For 10 servings: If using a blender, blend ingredients half at a time. Stir mixture together after blending.

To tote: Transport in an insulated cooler with ice packs. Place vegetable dippers in an airtight bag or container to transport.

NUTRITION FACTS PER SERVING: 209 cal., 10 g total fat (1 g sat. fat), 0 mg chol., 401 mg sodium, 24 g carbo., 7 g fiber, 8 g pro.
DAILY VALUES: 227% vit. A, 200% vit. C, 8% calcium, 11% iron

Queso Fondue with Corn Bread Dippers

Of course you can use cubes of bread for dipping, but the corn bread dippers are perfect partners for this delicious fondue.

PREP: 45 minutes BAKE: 28 minutes
COOL: 1 hour OVEN: 400°F

48 SERVINGS	INGREDIENTS	24 SERVINGS
1 8¹/₂-oz. pkg.	corn muffin mix	1 8¹/₂-oz. pkg.
3 cups (12 oz.)	shredded Monterey Jack cheese	1¹/₂ cups (6 oz.)
2 Tbsp.	all-purpose flour	1 Tbsp.
¹/₃ cup	finely chopped onion	3 Tbsp.
1 Tbsp.	butter or margarine	1¹/₂ tsp.
³/₄ cup	half-and-half or light cream	¹/₃ cup
2 4-oz. cans	diced green chile peppers, drained	1 4-oz. can
¹/₃ cup	chopped roasted red sweet peppers	3 Tbsp.
¹/₃ cup	finely chopped, peeled jicama	3 Tbsp.

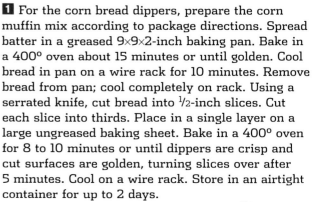

1 For the corn bread dippers, prepare the corn muffin mix according to package directions. Spread batter in a greased 9×9×2-inch baking pan. Bake in a 400° oven about 15 minutes or until golden. Cool bread in pan on a wire rack for 10 minutes. Remove bread from pan; cool completely on rack. Using a serrated knife, cut bread into ¹/₂-inch slices. Cut each slice into thirds. Place in a single layer on a large ungreased baking sheet. Bake in a 400° oven for 8 to 10 minutes or until dippers are crisp and cut surfaces are golden, turning slices over after 5 minutes. Cool on a wire rack. Store in an airtight container for up to 2 days.

2 For fondue, toss together cheese a⌃⌃⌃⌃⌃⌃ ⌃⌃t aside. In a medium saucepan cook onion in hot butter until tender; stir in half-and-half. Gradually add small amounts of the cheese mixture, stirring constantly over low heat until cheese is melted. Stir in chile peppers, roasted sweet peppers, and jicama; heat through. Transfer to a fondue pot; keep warm over a fondue burner.

For 24 dippers: After cooling corn bread, reserve half for another use. Cut remaining; bake as above.

To tote: Cover fondue tightly. Transport in an insulated carrier. Transfer to a fondue pot or slow cooker to serve. Transport dippers in an airtight container.

NUTRITION FACTS PER DIPPER (WITH 2 TEASPOONS SAUCE): 60 cal., 4 g total fat (2 g sat. fat), 12 mg chol., 101 mg sodium, 5 g carbo., 0 g fiber, 2 g pro. DAILY VALUES: 2% vit. A, 8% vit. C, 7% calcium, 1% iron

Spicy Artichoke Dip

For a festive presentation, serve with red and green tortilla chips instead of baguette slices.

1 In a large bowl combine chopped artichoke hearts, mayonnaise, Parmesan cheese, green chile peppers, pickled jalapeño peppers, cumin, and garlic. Spoon artichoke mixture into an ungreased 1¹/₂-quart casserole. Sprinkle with paprika.

2 Bake, uncovered, in a 350° oven about 30 minutes or until hot and bubbly. Let stand about 10 minutes before serving. (If toting, see below.) Serve with chips.

For 14 servings: Prepare using method above, except spoon into a 2- to 3-cup casserole and bake about 25 minutes.

To tote: Do not let stand after baking. Cover tightly. Transport in an insulated carrier. Pack chips in an airtight bag or container.

NUTRITION FACTS PER SERVING: 132 cal., 9 g total fat (2 g sat. fat), 4 mg chol., 261 mg sodium, 11 g carbo., 2 g fiber, 3 g pro.
DAILY VALUES: 2% vit. A, 3% vit. C, 7% calcium, 5% iron

PREP: 25 minutes BAKE: 30 minutes
STAND: 10 minutes OVEN: 350°F

40 SERVINGS — INGREDIENTS — 14 SERVINGS

40 SERVINGS	INGREDIENTS	14 SERVINGS
3 14-oz. cans	artichoke hearts, rinsed, drained, and coarsely chopped	1 14-oz. can
1 cup	mayonnaise or salad dressing	¹/₃ cup
1 cup	grated Parmesan cheese	¹/₃ cup
1 4-oz. can	diced green chile peppers, drained	2 Tbsp.
2 Tbsp.	drained and chopped pickled jalapeño peppers	2 tsp.
¹/₂ tsp.	ground cumin	¹/₈ tsp.
3 cloves	garlic, minced	1 clove
	Paprika	
	Toasted baguette slices	

Chilly Veggie Pizza

This recipe is perfect for all occasions. It's an appetizer, a main dish, or a light lunch. Part of this pizza's appeal comes from the variety of vegetables on top of the cool crust covered with cream cheese.

PREP: 30 minutes BAKE: 8 minutes
CHILL: 2 to 4 hours OVEN: 375°F

12 SERVINGS — INGREDIENTS — 6 SERVINGS

12 SERVINGS	INGREDIENTS	6 SERVINGS
1 8-oz. pkg.	refrigerated crescent rolls	1 4-oz. pkg.
1 8-oz. pkg.	cream cheese, softened	1/2 8-oz. pkg.
1/3 cup	mayonnaise or salad dressing	3 Tbsp.
2 Tbsp.	thinly sliced green onion	1 Tbsp.
1/2 tsp.	dried dill	1/4 tsp.
1/2 cup	shredded lettuce	1/4 cup
1/3 cup	sliced pimiento-stuffed green olives or pitted ripe olives	3 Tbsp.
1/4 cup	chopped green and/or yellow sweet pepper	2 Tbsp.
1/4 cup	chopped seeded cucumber	2 Tbsp.
1 medium	tomato, seeded and chopped	1 small
2/3 cup	crumbled garlic-and-herb feta cheese	1/3 cup

1 Unroll crescent rolls. Press the dough into a greased 12-inch pizza pan or over the bottom and about 1/2 inch up the sides of a lightly greased 13×9×2-inch baking pan; press dough perforations to seal. Bake in a 375° oven for 8 to 10 minutes or until light brown. Cool.

2 Meanwhile, in a medium bowl combine the cream cheese, mayonnaise, green onion, and dill. Spread cream cheese mixture over cooled crust. Top with the lettuce, olives, sweet pepper, cucumber, and tomato. Sprinkle with feta cheese. Cover and chill for up to 4 hours.

For 6 servings: Prepare using method above, except press dough into a lightly greased 8×8×2-inch baking pan.

To tote: Transport pizza in an insulated cooler with ice packs.

NUTRITION FACTS PER SERVING: 206 cal., 17 g total fat (7 g sat. fat), 28 mg chol., 334 mg sodium, 9 g carbo., 0 g fiber, 4 g pro.
DAILY VALUES: 8% vit. A, 7% vit. C, 5% calcium, 5% iron

Easy Vegetable Dip

What's great about this dip—other than its flavor— is how quickly it goes together. When you have an after-work party to attend, blend the ingredients while you're home for lunch, cover and refrigerate the dip, then pick it up on your way to the party.

PREP: 15 minutes   CHILL: 2 to 48 hours

18 SERVINGS · INGREDIENTS · 6 SERVINGS

18 SERVINGS	INGREDIENTS	6 SERVINGS
1 cup	mayonnaise or salad dressing	1/3 cup
1 8-oz. carton	dairy sour cream	1/3 cup
6	green onions, cut into 3-inch pieces	2
6 sprigs	fresh parsley, stems removed	2 sprigs
1/4 tsp.	garlic powder	Dash
	Assorted vegetable dippers (such as red sweet pepper, broccoli florets, cauliflowerets, or carrot sticks) and/or crackers	

1 In a food processor bowl or blender container combine mayonnaise, sour cream, green onions, parsley, and garlic powder. Cover and process or blend until smooth. Cover and chill for 2 to 48 hours. Serve with vegetable dippers and/or crackers.

To tote: Transport dip and vegetable dippers in an insulated cooler with ice packs. Pack crackers in an airtight bag or container.

NUTRITION FACTS PER SERVING: 137 cal., 13 g total fat (3 g sat. fat), 13 mg chol., 94 mg sodium, 6 g carbo., 2 g fiber, 2 g pro.
DAILY VALUES: 137% vit. A, 83% vit. C, 4% calcium, 3% iron

Tortellini, Olive, and Cheese Kabobs

If you like, you can serve this recipe in a bowl rather than as kabobs. Have plenty of toothpicks available for spearing.

1 For marinade, in a medium bowl combine salad dressing and pesto; set aside.

2 Meanwhile, cook tortellini according to package directions; drain. Rinse with cold water; drain again.

3 On 15 (or eight) 6-inch picks or skewers, alternately thread the cooked tortellini, cheese cubes, olives, and pickled peppers. Place kabobs in a 13×9×2-inch baking dish. Brush with marinade. Cover and chill for 3 to 4 hours.

To tote: Transport kabobs in an insulated cooler with ice packs.

NUTRITION FACTS PER SERVING: 74 cal., 4 g total fat (2 g sat. fat), 9 mg chol., 293 mg sodium, 5 g carbo., 1 g fiber, 3 g pro.
DAILY VALUES: 6% vit. A, 7% calcium, 1% iron

PREP: 25 minutes   CHILL: 3 to 4 hours

15 SERVINGS / INGREDIENTS / 8 SERVINGS

15 SERVINGS	INGREDIENTS	8 SERVINGS
2/3 cup	bottled oil-and-vinegar salad dressing	1/3 cup
3 Tbsp.	purchased basil pesto	5 tsp.
2 cups	frozen cheese-filled tortellini	1 cup
8 oz.	cheddar cheese and/or Monterey Jack cheese with jalapeño peppers, cut into 1/2- to 3/4-inch cubes	4 oz.
30	assorted pitted olives (such as ripe or kalamata olives or pimiento-stuffed olives)	16
30	red or green pickled jalapeño peppers	16

Sweet, Hot, and Sour Meatballs

If kids are on the guest list, apple juice is a fine substitute for the whiskey in these tasty sausage and beef meatballs.

1 In a large bowl combine egg product, bread crumbs, onion, milk, salt, and pepper. Add sausage and beef; mix well. Shape into 48 meatballs. Place meatballs in a shallow baking pan. Bake, uncovered, in a 375° oven about 30 minutes or until done (160°). Remove from oven; drain.

2 Meanwhile, in a large saucepan stir together jelly, mustard, whiskey, Worcestershire sauce, and bottled hot pepper sauce. Heat and stir until jelly melts and mixture bubbles. Add meatballs, stirring gently to coat. Cook for 3 to 5 minutes or until sauce thickens slightly and meatballs are coated.

To tote: Transfer meatballs and sauce to a serving dish; cover tightly. Transport in an insulated carrier.

NUTRITION FACTS PER SERVING: 154 cal., 8 g total fat (3 g sat. fat), 23 mg chol., 232 mg sodium, 9 g carbo., 0 g fiber, 7 g pro.
DAILY VALUES: 1% vit. C, 2% calcium, 4% iron

PREP: 20 minutes
BAKE: 30 minutes OVEN: 375°F

24 SERVINGS	INGREDIENTS	6 SERVINGS
1/2 cup	refrigerated or frozen egg product, thawed	2 Tbsp.
1/2 cup	fine dry bread crumbs	2 Tbsp.
1/2 cup	finely chopped onion	2 Tbsp.
1/4 cup	milk	1 Tbsp.
1/2 tsp.	salt	1/8 tsp.
1/2 tsp.	black pepper	1/8 tsp.
1 lb.	bulk pork sausage	4 oz.
1 lb.	ground beef	4 oz.
3/4 cup	apple jelly	3 Tbsp.
1/3 cup	spicy brown mustard	4 tsp.
1/3 cup	whiskey or apple juice	4 tsp.
1 1/2 tsp.	Worcestershire sauce	1/2 tsp.
Few dashes	bottled hot pepper sauce	Dash

Mini Meat Turnovers

In Mexico, these meat-filled turnovers are known as empañaditas. *Refrigerated biscuits replace the homemade pastry traditionally used, simplifying preparation.*

1 For filling, in a large skillet cook ground beef until brown; drain off fat. Stir in tomato sauce, chili powder, oregano, and garlic powder. Bring to boiling; reduce heat. Simmer, uncovered, for 5 minutes. Remove from heat. Stir in cilantro.

2 Grease a large baking sheet; set aside. Separate biscuits; cut each biscuit in half horizontally. On a lightly floured surface, roll each piece of biscuit dough into a 4-inch circle. Place about 1 tablespoon filling onto half of each circle. Fold opposite side of circle up and over filling. Brush edges with a little milk; seal edges with a fork.

3 Place filled turnovers 1 inch apart on prepared baking sheet; brush with milk. Bake in a 350° oven for 10 to 12 minutes or until golden brown. Immediately remove from baking sheet. Cool slightly on a wire rack. Serve warm. If desired, serve with salsa for dipping.

Make-ahead directions: Cool turnovers completely on wire racks. Place in an airtight freezer container; freeze for up to 3 months. To reheat, transfer frozen turnovers to an ungreased cookie sheet. Bake, uncovered, in a 350° oven for 10 to 12 minutes or until heated through.

To tote: Cover hot turnovers tightly. Transport in an insulated carrier.

Test Kitchen Tip: If making the 40-turnover recipe, remove only one package of biscuits from the refrigerator at a time.

NUTRITION FACTS PER TURNOVER: 60 cal., 2 g total fat (1 g sat. fat), 9 mg chol., 175 mg sodium, 7 g carbo., 0 g fiber, 4 g pro.
DAILY VALUES: 1% vit. A, 4% iron

PREP: 50 minutes BAKE: 10 minutes per batch
OVEN: 350°F

40 SERVINGS	INGREDIENTS	20 SERVINGS
1¼ lb.	lean ground beef	12 oz.
1 15-oz. can	tomato sauce	1 8-oz. can
2 tsp.	chili powder	1 tsp.
2 tsp.	dried oregano, crushed	1 tsp.
1 tsp.	garlic powder	½ tsp.
1 Tbsp.	snipped fresh cilantro	1½ tsp.
2 10- to 12-oz. pkgs. (20)	refrigerated buttermilk biscuits	1 10- to 12-oz. pkg. (10)
	Milk	
	Salsa (optional)	

Sweet and Sour Chicken Wings

These chicken wings, sweetly glazed with pineapple juice, catsup, and soy sauce, are a can't-miss choice to take to potlucks.

PREP: 20 minutes
BAKE: 30 minutes   OVEN: 350°F

24 SERVINGS	INGREDIENTS	12 SERVINGS
2½ lb.	chicken wings	1¼ lb.
½ cup	all-purpose flour	¼ cup
½ tsp.	lemon-pepper seasoning	¼ tsp.
¼ tsp.	garlic salt	⅛ tsp.
3 Tbsp.	cooking oil	4½ tsp.
⅔ cup	sugar	⅓ cup
½ cup	white wine vinegar or rice vinegar	¼ cup
¼ cup	unsweetened pineapple juice	2 Tbsp.
¼ cup	catsup	2 Tbsp.
1 tsp.	soy sauce	½ tsp.
	Green onions (optional)	

1 Cut off and discard tips of chicken wings. Cut wings at joints to form 24 to 30 pieces.

2 In a shallow dish combine flour, lemon-pepper seasoning, and garlic salt. Coat each chicken piece with the flour mixture.

3 Heat oil in a 12-inch skillet. Add coated chicken pieces to skillet. Cook, uncovered, until brown, turning occasionally. Remove chicken from skillet and arrange in a 3-quart rectangular baking dish.

4 In a medium saucepan whisk together sugar, vinegar, pineapple juice, catsup, and soy sauce. Bring to boiling, stirring to dissolve sugar; pour over chicken. Bake, uncovered, in a 350° oven about 30 minutes or until chicken is tender and no longer pink, turning pieces over after 15 minutes. If desired, garnish with green onions.

For 12 servings: Prepare using method above, except brown chicken in a 10-inch skillet and bake in a 2-quart rectangular baking dish.

To tote: Cover tightly. Transport chicken wings and, if desired, green onions in an insulated carrier.

NUTRITION FACTS PER PIECE: 153 cal., 9 g total fat (2 g sat. fat), 36 mg chol., 108 mg sodium, 9 g carbo., 0 g fiber, 9 g pro.
DAILY VALUES: 2% vit. A, 2% vit. C, 1% calcium, 3% iron

Crunchy Cracker Snack Mix

Customize this snack mix by substituting some of your favorite bite-size crackers. Also, if you prefer a particular type of nut, substitute it for the mixed nuts.

PREP: 10 minutes
BAKE: 25 minutes   OVEN: 300°F

52 SERVINGS — INGREDIENTS — 12 SERVINGS

52 Servings	Ingredients	12 Servings
4 cups	bite-size cheese crackers	1 cup
5 cups	snack sticks	1 1/4 cups
3 cups	pretzel twists	3/4 cup
2 cups	mixed nuts	1/2 cup
1/2 cup	butter or margarine, melted	2 Tbsp.
1 7-oz. env.	cheese-garlic, Parmesan, or Italian dry salad dressing mix	1/4 7-oz. env. (2 1/4 tsp.)

1 Place cheese crackers and snack sticks in a large roasting pan. Bake in a 300° oven about 5 minutes or until warm. Stir in pretzel twists and nuts. Pour melted butter over all. Sprinkle with salad dressing mix; stir to coat.

2 Bake for 20 minutes more, stirring once. Spread snack mix on foil to cool. Store in an airtight container for up to 1 week.

For 12 servings: Prepare using method above, except bake snack mix in an 8×8×2-inch or 9×9×2-inch baking pan.

To tote: Transport in an airtight container.

NUTRITION FACTS PER 1/4-CUP SERVING: 108 cal., 7 g total fat (2 g sat. fat), 5 mg chol., 217 mg sodium, 10 g carbo., 1 g fiber, 2 g pro.
DAILY VALUES: 2% vit. A, 1% calcium, 3% iron

Tequila Shrimp with Dried Tomato Mayo

Dunk marinated shrimp in a garlic-and-tomato mayonnaise for an unforgettable appetizer. Use precooked shrimp to make this recipe even easier.

PREP: 30 minutes
MARINATE: 2 hours   CHILL: 2 hours

INGREDIENTS

12 SERVINGS		6 SERVINGS
1 lb.	fresh or frozen large shrimp in shells, peeled and deveined (leave tails intact, if desired)	8 oz.
1/2 cup	tequila*	1/4 cup
1/4 cup	finely chopped onion	2 Tbsp.
1/4 cup	lime juice	2 Tbsp.
2 Tbsp.	snipped fresh cilantro or parsley	1 Tbsp.
2 Tbsp.	olive oil	1 Tbsp.
1/2 cup	dried tomatoes (not oil packed)	1/4 cup
1 cup	mayonnaise or salad dressing	1/2 cup
1 Tbsp.	snipped fresh cilantro or parsley	1 1/2 tsp.
1 Tbsp.	milk	1 1/2 tsp.
1 tsp.	bottled minced garlic	1/2 tsp.
1/8 tsp.	salt	Dash
	Crushed ice	
	Lime wedges	

1 Thaw shrimp, if frozen. In a large saucepan cook shrimp, uncovered, in boiling lightly salted water for 2 to 3 minutes or until shrimp turn opaque; drain. Rinse under cold running water; drain again. Place shrimp in a heavy plastic bag set in a shallow dish.

2 For marinade, in a bowl combine tequila, onion, lime juice, the 2 tablespoons cilantro, and olive oil. Pour marinade over shrimp; seal bag. Marinate in the refrigerator for 2 hours, turning bag occasionally.

3 For mayonnaise mixture, in a small bowl cover dried tomatoes with boiling water; let stand for 5 minutes. Drain well. Finely chop tomatoes. In a small bowl combine chopped tomatoes, mayonnaise, the 1 tablespoon cilantro, milk, garlic, and salt. Transfer to a serving bowl. Cover and chill about 2 hours or until ready to serve.

4 To serve, drain shrimp, discarding marinade. Transfer to serving bowl. Place serving bowl in a larger bowl filled with crushed ice. Serve with mayonnaise mixture and lime wedges.

To tote: Transport shrimp, mayonnaise mixture, and lime wedges in an insulated cooler with ice packs.

*NOTE: For a nonalcoholic version, omit the tequila from the marinade.

NUTRITION FACTS PER SERVING: 220 cal., 19 g total fat (3 g sat. fat), 60 mg chol., 258 mg sodium, 3 g carbo., 0 g fiber, 7 g pro.
DAILY VALUES: 3% vit. A, 5% vit. C, 3% calcium, 6% iron

Shrimp with Mustard Cream Sauce

Oh-so-elegant describes these tasty shrimp. If you're short on time, omit the snow peas.

1 Thaw shrimp, if frozen. In a large saucepan cook shrimp and snow peas, uncovered, in boiling lightly salted water about 2 minutes or until shrimp turn opaque; drain. Rinse under cold running water; drain again. Cool. Wrap a snow pea around each shrimp. Secure with a wooden toothpick. Cover and chill for 2 to 24 hours.

2 For sauce, in a small bowl stir together sour cream, mustard, milk, and pepper. Cover and chill for 2 to 24 hours.

3 To serve, sprinkle sauce with capers. Serve shrimp with sauce on a bed of Romaine leaves, if desired.

To tote: Transport shrimp and sauce in an insulated cooler with ice packs.

NUTRITION FACTS PER SERVING: 109 cal., 5 g total fat (3 g sat. fat), 95 mg chol., 131 mg sodium, 2 g carbo., 0 g fiber, 12 g pro.
DAILY VALUES: 5% vit. A, 3% vit. C, 6% calcium, 9% iron

PREP: 25 minutes   CHILL: 2 to 24 hours

12 SERVINGS — INGREDIENTS — 6 SERVINGS

12 SERVINGS	INGREDIENTS	6 SERVINGS
1½ lb.	fresh or frozen medium shrimp in shells, peeled and deveined (leave tails intact, if desired)	12 oz.
36	fresh snow peas	18
1 8-oz. carton	dairy sour cream	½ cup
2 Tbsp.	Dijon-style mustard	1 Tbsp.
2 tsp.	milk	1 tsp.
½ tsp.	black pepper	¼ tsp.
1 Tbsp.	capers, drained	1½ tsp.
	Romaine leaves (optional)	

CHAPTER 2

FAVORITE POULTRY DISHES

RECIPE FINDER

FOR MORE RECIPES:

Visit our Recipe Center at www.bhg.com/bkrecipe

p. 35   p. 38

p. 42   p. 46

p. 48   p. 58

Baked Chicken Marsala, p. 56

Chicken Antipasto Salad

These classic antipasto ingredients—artichoke hearts, kalamata olives, and tomatoes—are dressed with an olive oil vinaigrette for a tasty picnic dish.

PREP: 40 minutes   CHILL: 1 to 6 hours

12 SERVINGS	INGREDIENTS	6 SERVINGS
2 9-oz. pkgs.	refrigerated cheese-filled tortellini	1 9-ounce pkg.
1/2 cup	olive oil	1/4 cup
1/2 cup	red wine vinegar	1/4 cup
2 Tbsp.	sugar	1 Tbsp.
2 Tbsp.	Dijon-style mustard	1 Tbsp.
1/2 tsp.	dried basil, crushed	1/4 tsp.
1/4 tsp.	black pepper	1/8 tsp.
4 cloves	garlic, minced	2 cloves
2 9-oz. pkgs.	frozen cooked chicken breast strips, thawed, OR	1 9-oz. pkg.
4 cups	cooked chicken breast strips*	2 cups
2 15-oz. cans	chickpeas (garbanzo beans), rinsed and drained	1 15-oz. can
2 14-oz. cans	artichoke hearts, drained and quartered	1 14-oz. can
1 cup	thinly sliced red onion	1/2 cup
1/2 cup	pitted whole kalamata olives or ripe olives, drained and halved	1/4 cup
2 cups	coarsely chopped tomatoes	1 cup

1 Cook tortellini according to package directions; drain. Rinse with cold water; drain again. Place tortellini in a very large bowl; set aside.

2 Meanwhile, for dressing, in a screw-top jar combine the oil, vinegar, sugar, mustard, basil, pepper, and garlic. Cover and shake well.

3 Add chicken strips, chickpeas, artichokes, onion, and olives to tortellini in bowl; stir gently. Add the dressing, tossing gently to coat. Cover and chill for at least 1 hour or up to 6 hours, stirring occasionally. Just before serving, gently stir in chopped tomatoes.

To tote: Transport salad and chopped tomatoes in an insulated cooler with ice packs.

*NOTE: About 1 1/2 pounds boneless chicken breasts will yield 4 cups cooked chicken strips; 12 ounces will yield 2 cups cooked chicken strips.

NUTRITION FACTS PER SERVING: 406 cal., 16 g total fat (3 g sat. fat), 50 mg chol., 907 mg sodium, 45 g carbo., 6 g fiber, 22 g pro.
DAILY VALUES: 6% vit. A, 18% vit. C, 13% calcium, 20% iron

Wild Rice-Chicken Salad

A convenient wild rice mix supplies the base for this easy salad. Choices for dressing are many. Check your supermarket shelf for any oil-and-vinegar variety.

1 Cook rice mix according to package directions.

2 In a large bowl combine the cooked rice, snow peas, chicken, and sweet pepper strips. Pour salad dressing over rice mixture; stir gently to coat. Cover and chill for 2 to 8 hours.

3 Place the green onion strips in ice water for 20 minutes; drain well. To serve, arrange green onions around the edge of a large serving platter. Spoon salad into center.

To tote: Transport salad and green onions in an insulated cooler with ice packs. Just before serving, transfer green onions and salad to a serving platter.

NUTRITION FACTS PER SERVING: 407 cal., 10 g total fat (2 g sat. fat), 93 mg chol., 1,780 mg sodium, 43 g carbo., 2 g fiber, 37 g pro.
DAILY VALUES: 36% vit. A, 121% vit. C, 5% calcium, 19% iron

PREP: 35 minutes   CHILL: 2 to 8 hours

8 SERVINGS — INGREDIENTS — 4 SERVINGS

8 SERVINGS	INGREDIENTS	4 SERVINGS
2 6.2-oz. pkgs.	quick-cooking long grain and wild rice mix	1 6.2-oz. pkg.
3 cups	snow peas, tips and strings removed	1$^{1}/_{2}$ cups
6 cups	coarsely chopped cooked chicken	3 cups
2 medium	red sweet peppers, cut into thin, bite-size strips	1 medium
1$^{1}/_{4}$ cups	bottled lemon-pepper salad dressing or vinaigrette salad dressing	$^{2}/_{3}$ cup
10	green onions, cut into thin strips	5

Ginger-Chicken Pasta Salad

The flavors of Asia dominate in this pasta salad. Its fresh and colorful appearance will be a welcome addition to any potluck table.

1 Cook pasta according to package directions; drain. Rinse with cold water; drain again.

2 Meanwhile, cook snow peas in boiling water for 30 seconds. Drain; rinse with cold water. Cover and chill until serving time.

3 For dressing, in a screw-top jar combine oil, vinegar, sugar, soy sauce, ginger, and crushed red pepper. Cover and shake well.

4 In a very large bowl combine cooked pasta, chicken, sweet pepper strips, radishes, green onions, and cilantro. Add dressing; toss gently to coat. Cover and chill for 4 to 24 hours.

5 Just before serving, add pea pods to salad; toss to mix and coat with dressing. Sprinkle salad with peanuts.

To tote: Transport salad, pea pods, and peanuts in an insulated cooler with ice packs.

NUTRITION FACTS PER SERVING: 484 cal., 20 g total fat (3 g sat. fat), 50 mg chol., 492 mg sodium, 48 g carbo., 5 g fiber, 28 g pro.
DAILY VALUES: 57% vit. A, 156% vit. C, 6% calcium, 17% iron

PREP: 35 minutes   CHILL: 4 to 24 hours

12 SERVINGS	INGREDIENTS	6 SERVINGS
1 lb.	dried rotini or small bow ties	8 oz.
3 cups	snow peas, tips and strings removed	1¹/₂ cups
¹/₃ cup	salad oil	3 Tbsp.
¹/₃ cup	rice vinegar	3 Tbsp.
¹/₄ cup	sugar	2 Tbsp.
¹/₄ cup	soy sauce	2 Tbsp.
1 Tbsp.	grated fresh ginger	1¹/₂ tsp.
1 tsp.	crushed red pepper	¹/₂ tsp.
4 cups	bite-size strips cooked chicken	2 cups
3 cups	yellow and/or red sweet pepper strips	1¹/₂ cups
1¹/₂ cups	thinly sliced radishes	³/₄ cup
1 cup	bias-sliced green onions	¹/₂ cup
¹/₃ cup	snipped fresh cilantro or parsley	3 Tbsp.
1 cup	chopped peanuts	¹/₂ cup

Chicken and Vegetable Salad

This unlikely blend of vegetables is a popular salad for those who like spicy food. Hot pepper sauce, cumin, jalapeño, and lime transform mayonnaise into a delicious dressing for the salad.

PREP: 35 minutes
CHILL: 6 hours or overnight

INGREDIENTS

8 SERVINGS		4 SERVINGS
2 lb.	skinless, boneless chicken breast halves and/or thighs	1 lb.
2 cups	cubed, peeled potatoes	1 cup
2 cups	sliced carrots	1 cup
2 cups	sliced zucchini	1 cup
1 10-oz. pkg.	frozen peas	1/2 10-oz. pkg.
1 cup	mayonnaise or salad dressing	1/2 cup
1/2 cup	pickled jalapeño pepper slices (reserve 2 Tbsp. juice)	1/4 cup
2 Tbsp.	lime juice	1 Tbsp.
1 tsp.	ground cumin	1/2 tsp.
1/4 tsp.	salt	1/8 tsp.
4 dashes	bottled hot pepper sauce	2 dashes
2	large tomatoes, peeled and coarsely chopped	1
4 cups	shredded lettuce	2 cups
	Sliced radishes (optional)	

1 In a large skillet place chicken and enough water to cover. Bring to boiling; reduce heat. Simmer, covered, for 12 to 14 minutes or until chicken is no longer pink (170° for breasts, 180° for thighs). Drain well. Cool chicken; cut into cubes (you should have about 2 1/2 cups).

2 Meanwhile, in a large saucepan cook potatoes and carrots in boiling salted water about 10 minutes or until crisp-tender, adding zucchini and frozen peas during the last 3 to 5 minutes of cooking. Drain and cool.

3 For dressing, in a small bowl stir together mayonnaise, reserved jalapeño juice, lime juice, cumin, salt, and hot pepper sauce.

4 In a large bowl combine chicken, potatoes, carrots, zucchini, peas, and tomatoes. Gently fold in dressing. Cover and chill for 6 hours or overnight.

5 To serve, line a large serving platter with lettuce. Spoon salad over lettuce. Top with jalapeño slices. If desired, garnish with radishes.

To tote: Transport salad, lettuce, jalapeño slices, and, if desired, radishes in an insulated cooler with ice packs. Just before serving, transfer lettuce and salad to a serving platter; add toppings.

NUTRITION FACTS PER SERVING: 418 cal., 24 g total fat (4 g sat. fat), 76 mg chol., 486 mg sodium, 19 g carbo., 5 g fiber, 30 g pro.
DAILY VALUES: 171% vit. A, 45% vit. C, 5% calcium, 14% iron

Chinese-Style Pasta Salad

Pasta steps in for steamed rice in this Asian-inspired salad. Be sure to purchase an Asian salad dressing to stay true to the salad's intended flavor.

1 Cook fettuccine according to package directions; drain. Rinse with cold water; drain again. Transfer fettuccine to a very large bowl. Stir in chicken, celery, green onions, and cilantro. Pour dressing over all; toss to coat well. Cover and chill for 4 to 24 hours. Just before serving, sprinkle with sesame seeds.

To tote: Transport salad and sesame seeds in an insulated cooler with ice packs.

*NOTE: About 1¹/₂ pounds boneless chicken breasts will yield 4 cups chopped cooked chicken; 12 ounces boneless chicken breasts will yield 2 cups chopped cooked chicken.

NUTRITION FACTS PER SERVING: 399 cal., 9 g total fat (2 g sat. fat), 62 mg chol., 754 mg sodium, 48 g carbo., 2 g fiber, 29 g pro.
DAILY VALUES: 5% vit. A, 6% vit. C, 4% calcium, 16% iron

PREP: 25 minutes CHILL: 4 to 24 hours

12 SERVINGS	INGREDIENTS	6 SERVINGS
1 16-oz. pkg.	dried fettuccine or linguine	8 oz.
4 cups	chopped cooked chicken*	2 cups
1¹/₂ cups	thinly bias-sliced celery	³/₄ cup
¹/₂ cup	sliced green onions	¹/₄ cup
¹/₄ cup	snipped fresh cilantro or parsley	2 Tbsp.
1 8-oz. bottle	Asian vinaigrette salad dressing	¹/₂ cup bottled
2 tsp.	sesame seeds, toasted	1 tsp.

Hot Chicken Salad

This hot chicken salad derives its creaminess from sour cream, mozzarella cheese, and cream of chicken soup. Serve over slices of French bread.

PREP: 30 minutes BAKE: 30 minutes
STAND: 10 minutes OVEN: 400°F

12 SERVINGS — INGREDIENTS — 6 SERVINGS

12 SERVINGS	INGREDIENTS	6 SERVINGS
1 cup	coarsely crushed potato chips	1/2 cup
2/3 cup	finely chopped almonds	1/3 cup
6 cups	cubed cooked chicken*	3 cups
3 cups	chopped celery	1 1/2 cups
1 10 3/4-oz. can	condensed cream of chicken soup	1 10 3/4-oz. can
2 cups (8 oz.)	shredded mozzarella cheese	1 cup (4 oz.)
2 8-oz. cartons	dairy sour cream or plain yogurt	1 8-oz. carton
1/4 cup	chopped onion	2 Tbsp.
1 tsp.	dried thyme or basil, crushed	1/2 tsp.
4	hard-cooked eggs, chopped	2

1 In a small bowl combine potato chips and almonds; set aside. In a very large bowl combine chicken, celery, soup, cheese, sour cream, onion, and thyme. Gently fold in hard-cooked eggs. Transfer to a 3-quart rectangular baking dish. Sprinkle with potato chip mixture.

2 Bake, uncovered, in a 400° oven for 30 to 35 minutes or until heated through. Let stand for 10 minutes before serving (If toting, see below).

For 6 servings: Prepare as above, except stir ingredients together in a large bowl and transfer to a 2-quart square baking dish.

To tote: Do not let stand after baking. Cover tightly. Transport in an insulated carrier.

***NOTE:** About 2 1/4 pounds boneless chicken breasts will yield 6 cups chopped cooked chicken; about 1 pound will yield 3 cups chopped cooked chicken.

NUTRITION FACTS PER SERVING: 398 cal., 25 g total fat (10 g sat. fat), 168 mg chol., 437 mg sodium, 9 g carbo., 2 g fiber, 33 g pro.
DAILY VALUES: 14% vit. A, 8% vit. C, 22% calcium, 10% iron

Oriental Chicken Slaw

Ease of preparation makes this salad perfect for potlucks. Curly noodles, almonds, and rice vinegar dress up an ordinary coleslaw mixture.

1 For dressing, in a small bowl whisk together oil, vinegar, sugar, red pepper, and contents of seasoning packet(s) from ramen noodles. Set dressing aside.

2 In a large saucepan cook ramen noodles in boiling water for 2 to 3 minutes or just until tender; drain. Transfer noodles to a large bowl. Pour ¼ cup of the dressing over the cooked noodles; toss to coat. Add chicken, cabbage, almonds, and green onions to noodle mixture; mix well. Pour the remaining dressing over the salad; toss to combine. Cover and chill for 2 to 24 hours.

To tote: Transport salad in an insulated cooler with ice packs.

NUTRITION FACTS PER SERVING: 470 cal., 30 g total fat (4 g sat. fat), 63 mg chol., 445 mg sodium, 24 g carbo., 2 g fiber, 26 g pro.
DAILY VALUES: 2% vit. A, 22% vit. C, 7% calcium, 11% iron

PREP: 20 minutes   CHILL: 2 to 24 hours

8 SERVINGS	INGREDIENTS	4 SERVINGS
½ cup	salad oil	¼ cup
½ cup	rice vinegar	¼ cup
¼ cup	sugar	2 Tbsp.
¼ tsp.	crushed red pepper	⅛ tsp.
2 3-oz. pkgs.	chicken-flavored ramen noodles	1 3-oz. pkg.
4 cups	finely chopped cooked chicken	2 cups
4 cups	packaged shredded cabbage with carrot (coleslaw mix)	2 cups
¾ cup	sliced almonds, toasted	⅓ cup
½ cup	sliced green onions	¼ cup

Mexican-Style Chicken

Layered with tortilla strips, a tomatoey sauce, chicken, and cheddar cheese, this casserole will melt the hearts of Mexican food fans.

PREP: 20 minutes BAKE: 45 minutes
STAND: 10 minutes OVEN: 350°F

INGREDIENTS

8 SERVINGS		4 SERVINGS
2 10³/₄-oz. cans	reduced-sodium condensed cream of chicken soup	1 10³/₄-oz. can
1 10-oz. can	diced tomatoes with green chiles, undrained	¹/₂ 10-oz. can
³/₄ cup	chopped green sweet pepper	¹/₃ cup
¹/₂ cup	chopped onion	¹/₄ cup
1¹/₂ tsp.	chili powder	³/₄ tsp.
¹/₄ tsp.	black pepper	¹/₈ tsp.
12 6- or 7-inch	corn tortillas, cut into thin, bite-size strips	6 6- or 7-inch
3 cups	cubed cooked chicken*	1¹/₂ cups
1 8-oz. pkg. (2 cups)	shredded cheddar cheese	1 4-oz. pkg. (1 cup)
	Tomato slices (optional)	
	Sliced green onions (optional)	

1 Combine soup, tomatoes with chiles, sweet pepper, onion, chili powder, and black pepper; set aside.

2 To assemble, sprinkle about one-third of the tortilla strips over the bottom of an ungreased 3-quart rectangular baking dish. Layer half of the chicken over tortilla strips; spoon half of soup mixture on top. Sprinkle half of the cheese and another one-third of the tortilla strips over the soup mixture. Layer with remaining chicken, soup mixture, and tortilla strips.

3 Bake, uncovered, in a 350° oven about 45 minutes or until bubbly around edges and center is hot. Remove from oven; sprinkle with remaining cheese. Let stand 10 minutes before serving. If desired, top with sliced tomatoes and green onions.

For 4 servings: Prepare as above, except assemble in an ungreased 2-quart square baking dish. Bake, uncovered, in a 350° oven about 35 minutes or until bubbly around edges and center is hot.

To tote: Cover tightly after sprinkling with cheese. Transport in an insulated carrier. If desired, transport tomatoes and green onions in an insulated cooler with ice packs.

*NOTE: About 1 pound boneless chicken breasts will yield 3 cups cubed cooked chicken; ¹/₂ pound yields about 1¹/₂ cups cubed cooked chicken.

NUTRITION FACTS PER SERVING: 380 cal., 16 g total fat (7 g sat. fat), 83 mg chol., 702 mg sodium, 33 g carbo., 2 g fiber, 27 g pro.
DAILY VALUES: 14% vit. A, 23% vit. C, 27% calcium, 19% iron

Tortellini Vegetable Bake

Use refrigerated—not dried—tortellini for this chicken-pasta bake. Cream cheese and a little lemon juice add a slight tang to the creamy sauce.

1 Cook tortellini according to package directions, adding the sugar snap peas and the carrot during the last 1 minute of cooking; drain well.

2 Meanwhile, melt butter in a 12-inch skillet; add chicken and mushrooms. Cook and stir about 5 minutes or until chicken is no longer pink. Remove from skillet.

3 In a screw-top jar combine chicken broth, flour, oregano, garlic salt, and pepper. Cover and shake until smooth. Add to skillet along with milk. Cook and stir until thickened and bubbly; add cream cheese. Cook and stir until cream cheese is smooth. Remove from heat; stir in lemon juice. Stir in pasta mixture, chicken mixture, tomatoes, and sweet pepper. Transfer to an ungreased 3-quart rectangular baking dish.

4 Bake, covered, in a 350° oven about 30 minutes or until heated through. Before serving, sprinkle with Parmesan cheese.

For 4 servings: Prepare as above, except assemble and bake in a 2-quart square baking dish.

To tote: Transport in an insulated carrier.

NUTRITION FACTS PER SERVING: 420 cal., 18 g total fat (10 g sat. fat), 101 mg chol., 501 mg sodium, 37 g carbo., 1 g fiber, 28 g pro.
DAILY VALUES: 70% vit. A, 42% vit. C, 22% calcium, 15% iron

PREP: 30 minutes
BAKE: 30 minutes   OVEN: 350°F

8 SERVINGS	INGREDIENTS	4 SERVINGS
2 9-oz. pkgs.	refrigerated tortellini	1 9-oz. pkg.
1¹/₂ cups	sugar snap peas, trimmed and halved crosswise	³/₄ cup
¹/₂ cup	thinly sliced carrot	¹/₄ cup
1 Tbsp.	butter or margarine	2 tsp.
1 lb.	skinless, boneless chicken breast halves, cut into bite-size pieces	8 oz.
1 cup	sliced fresh mushrooms	¹/₂ cup
¹/₃ cup	chicken broth	3 Tbsp.
2 tsp.	all-purpose flour	1 tsp.
1¹/₂ tsp.	dried oregano, crushed	³/₄ tsp.
¹/₂ tsp.	garlic salt	¹/₄ tsp.
¹/₂ tsp.	black pepper	¹/₄ tsp.
1 cup	milk	¹/₂ cup
1 8-oz. pkg.	cream cheese, cubed and softened	¹/₂ 8-oz. pkg.
1 Tbsp.	lemon juice	1¹/₂ tsp.
1 cup	quartered cherry tomatoes	¹/₂ cup
¹/₂ cup	coarsely chopped red or green sweet pepper	¹/₄ cup
2 Tbsp.	grated Parmesan cheese	1 Tbsp.

Chicken and Herbed Dressing Casserole

This tasty dressing is prepared in a slow cooker, making it an easy dish to transport to a holiday party.

PREP: 25 minutes   COOK: 4½ to 4 hours

12 SERVINGS	INGREDIENTS	6 SERVINGS
4½ cups	sliced fresh mushrooms	3 cups
1 cup	sliced celery	¾ cup
1 cup	chopped onion	¾ cup
⅓ cup	butter or margarine	¼ cup
⅓ cup	snipped fresh basil	¼ cup
½ tsp.	black pepper	¼ tsp.
12 cups	dry bread cubes	8 cups
3 cups	coarsely chopped cooked chicken or turkey	2 cups
1 14-oz. can	chicken broth	1¼ cups
¾ cup	chopped pecans, toasted	½ cup

1 In a large skillet cook mushrooms, celery, and onion in hot butter over medium heat for 5 minutes. Remove from heat; stir in basil and pepper. Combine mushroom mixture, dry bread cubes, and cooked chicken. Add chicken broth to moisten, tossing gently. Spoon chicken mixture into a 5- to 6-quart slow cooker. Cover and cook on low-heat setting for 3½ to 4 hours. Just before serving, gently stir in nuts.

For 6 servings: Prepare as above, except use a 3½- to 4-quart slow cooker.

Test Kitchen Tip: To make 12 cups of dry bread cubes, cut 20 to 22 slices of bread into ½-inch cubes. (To make 8 cups of dry cubes, start with 13 to 14 slices of bread.) Spread cubes in a single layer in a large, shallow baking pan. Bake, uncovered, in a 300°F oven for 10 to 15 minutes or until dry, stirring twice; cool. (Bread will continue to dry and crisp as it cools.)

To tote: Transport slow cooker and nuts in an insulated carrier. (Or, if desired, transfer hot mixture to a serving dish. Cover tightly. Transport in an insulated carrier.)

NUTRITION FACTS PER SERVING: 356 cal., 18 g total fat (6 g sat. fat), 58 mg chol., 509 mg sodium, 29 g carbo., 3 g fiber, 20 g pro.
DAILY VALUES: 7% vit. A, 3% vit. C, 8% calcium, 15% iron

Tex-Mex Chicken 'n' Rice Casserole

Rice appears twice—as long grain and in a vermicelli mix—in this crowd pleaser. The supporting cast of ingredients, including chile peppers, chili powder, and cumin, contributes to the Tex-Mex flavor.

1 In a 3-quart saucepan cook onion in hot oil until tender. Stir in rice and vermicelli mix (including seasoning package) and uncooked long grain rice. Cook and stir for 2 minutes. Stir in broth and water. Bring to boiling; reduce heat. Simmer, covered, for 20 minutes (liquid will not be fully absorbed).

2 Transfer the rice mixture to a very large bowl. Stir in chicken, tomatoes, chile peppers, basil, chili powder, cumin, and black pepper. Transfer to a 3-quart casserole.

3 Bake, covered, in a 425° oven for 25 minutes. Uncover and sprinkle with cheese. Let stand for 5 minutes before serving.

For 6 servings: Prepare as above, except assemble in a 2-quart square baking dish. (One package of rice mix is correct for this amount.)

Make-ahead directions: Prepare casserole; cover and chill for up to 24 hours. Bake, covered, in a 425° oven about 40 minutes or until heated through. Uncover and sprinkle with cheese. Let stand for 5 minutes before serving.

To tote: Cover tightly after sprinkling with cheese. Transport in an insulated carrier.

NUTRITION FACTS PER SERVING: 287 cal., 10 g total fat (3 g sat. fat), 51 mg chol., 578 mg sodium, 28 g carbo., 2 g fiber, 21 g pro.
DAILY VALUES: 13% vit. A, 20% vit. C, 11% calcium, 13% iron

PREP: 20 minutes   BAKE: 25 minutes
STAND: 5 minutes   OVEN: 425°F

INGREDIENTS

12 SERVINGS		6 SERVINGS
1 cup	chopped onion	1/2 cup
2 Tbsp.	olive oil	1 Tbsp.
1 6.9-oz. pkg.	chicken-flavored rice and vermicelli mix	1 6.9-oz. pkg.
1 cup	uncooked long grain rice	1/3 cup
2 14-oz. cans	chicken broth	1 14-oz. can
2 1/2 cups	water	2 cups
4 cups	chopped cooked chicken	2 cups
4 medium	tomatoes, chopped	2 medium
1 4-oz. can	diced green chile peppers, drained	3 Tbsp.
2 tsp.	dried basil, crushed	1 tsp.
1 Tbsp.	chili powder	1 1/2 tsp.
1/4 tsp.	ground cumin	1/8 tsp.
1/4 tsp.	black pepper	1/8 tsp.
1 cup (4 oz.)	shredded cheddar cheese	1/2 cup (2 oz.)

Layered Chicken and Chile Casserole

Patterned after a popular Texas recipe, this irresistible main dish includes seasoned chicken layered with chile peppers, tortillas, sour cream sauce, and cheese.

PREP: 20 minutes   BAKE: 35 minutes
STAND: 10 minutes   OVEN: 350°F

INGREDIENTS

12 SERVINGS		6 SERVINGS
2	tomatillos	1
1 cup	chopped onion	1/2 cup
4 tsp.	chili powder	2 tsp.
2 cloves	garlic, minced	1 clove
2 Tbsp.	cooking oil	1 Tbsp.
2 10³/₄-oz. cans	condensed cream of chicken soup	1 10³/₄-oz. can
2 4-oz. cans	diced green chile peppers, drained	1 4-oz. can
2 4-oz. jars	diced pimientos, drained	1 4-oz. jar
1/2 cup	dairy sour cream	1/4 cup
12 6-inch	corn tortillas, torn	6 6-inch
3 cups	cubed cooked chicken	1¹/₂ cups
2 cups (16 oz.)	shredded Monterey Jack cheese	1 cup (8 oz.)
	Green salsa (optional)	

1 Remove and discard the thin, brown, papery husks from the tomatillos. Rinse tomatillos; finely chop (you should have about ¹/₂ cup). For sauce, in a medium saucepan cook chopped tomatillos, onion, chili powder, and garlic in hot oil over medium heat until vegetables are tender. Remove from heat; stir in soup, chile peppers, pimientos, and sour cream.

2 Spread ¹/₂ cup of the sauce in the bottom of a 3-quart rectangular baking dish. Arrange half of the torn corn tortillas over the sauce. Layer with half of the chicken, half of the remaining sauce, and half of the Monterey Jack cheese. Repeat layers.

3 Bake, covered, in a 350° oven for 35 to 40 minutes or until heated through. Let stand for 10 minutes before serving (if toting, see below). If desired, serve with green salsa.

For 6 servings: Prepare as above, except assemble in a 2-quart square baking dish.

To tote: Do not let stand after baking. Cover tightly. Transport in an insulated carrier. If desired, transport green salsa in an insulated cooler with ice packs.

NUTRITION FACTS PER SERVING: 297 cal., 16 g total fat (7 g sat. fat), 55 mg chol., 663 mg sodium, 20 g carbo., 3 g fiber, 19 g pro.
DAILY VALUES: 26% vit. A, 41% vit. C, 23% calcium, 11% iron

Turkey Manicott
with Chive
Cream Sauce

A simple cream cheese sauce makes these pasta shells filled with turkey and broccoli elegant enough for a special gathering. It also can be made up to 24 hours in advance.

PREP: 30 minutes
BAKE: 30 minutes OVEN: 350°F

6 SERVINGS	INGREDIENTS	4 SERVINGS
12	dried manicotti shells	8
1 8-oz. tub	cream cheese with chive and onion	2/3 cup
2/3 cup	milk	1/2 cup
1/4 cup	grated Romano or Parmesan cheese	3 Tbsp.
2 cups	chopped cooked turkey or chicken	1 1/3 cups
1 10-oz. pkg.	frozen chopped broccoli, thawed and drained	1/2 10-oz. pkg.
1 4-oz. jar	diced pimientos, drained	1 2-oz. jar
1/4 tsp.	black pepper	1/8 tsp.

1 Cook manicotti according to package directions; drain. Rinse with cold water; drain again. Cool manicotti in a single layer on a piece of greased foil.

2 Meanwhile, for sauce, in a heavy small saucepan heat cream cheese over medium-low heat until melted, stirring constantly. Slowly stir in milk until smooth. Stir in Romano cheese.

3 For filling, combine 3/4 cup of the sauce, the turkey, broccoli, pimientos, and pepper. Using a small spoon, carefully fill each manicotti shell with 1/4 to 1/3 cup filling.

4 Arrange filled shells in a 3-quart rectangular baking dish. Pour remaining sauce over shells. Bake, covered, in a 350° oven for 30 to 35 minutes or until heated through.

For 4 servings: Prepare as above, except use 1/2 cup of the sauce in the filling and arrange filled shells in a 2-quart rectangular baking dish.

To tote: Transport in an insulated carrier.

NUTRITION FACTS PER SERVING: 381 cal., 17 g total fat (10 g sat. fat), 78 mg chol., 256 mg sodium, 32 g carbo., 3 g fiber, 22 g pro.
DAILY VALUES: 38% vit. A, 66% vit. C, 15% calcium, 13% iron

Nacho Turkey Casserole

If you enjoy nachos with all the fixings, you'll love this no-fuss casserole. Prep in 15 minutes, bake in 30 minutes—voilà!

1 Lightly grease a 3-quart rectangular baking dish. Place 3 cups of the tortilla chips in bottom of dish. In a large bowl combine turkey, salsa, corn, sour cream, and flour; spoon over tortilla chips.

2 Bake, uncovered, in a 350° oven for 25 minutes. Sprinkle with remaining 2 cups tortilla chips and the cheese. Bake, uncovered, for 5 to 10 minutes more or until heated through. If desired, top with sliced jalapeño chile peppers.

For 4 servings: Prepare as above, except assemble in a 2-quart square baking dish and place 1¹/₂ cups tortilla chips in bottom of dish.

To tote: Cover casserole tightly. Transport in an insulated carrier.

NUTRITION FACTS PER SERVING: 444 cal., 17 g total fat (7 g sat. fat), 74 mg chol., 1,127 mg sodium, 46 g carbo., 4 g fiber, 29 g pro.
DAILY VALUES: 21% vit. A, 33% vit. C, 20% calcium, 11% iron

PREP: 15 minutes
BAKE: 30 minutes   OVEN: 350°F

INGREDIENTS

8 SERVINGS		4 SERVINGS
5 cups	slightly crushed tortilla chips	2¹/₂ cups
4 cups	cubed cooked turkey or chicken	2 cups
2 16-oz. jars	salsa	1 16-oz. jar
1 10-oz. pkg.	frozen whole kernel corn	1 cup
¹/₂ cup	dairy sour cream	¹/₄ cup
2 Tbsp.	all-purpose flour	1 Tbsp.
1 cup (4 oz.)	shredded Monterey Jack cheese with jalapeño peppers or mozzarella cheese	¹/₂ cup (2 oz.)
	Sliced jalapeño chile pepper, thinly sliced (optional)	

Turkey-Spinach Casserole

For a potluck or party, use the large baking dish. For a smaller party or dinner at home, the au gratin dishes are more elegant.

PREP: 30 minutes
BAKE: 25 minutes OVEN: 350°F

8 SERVINGS — INGREDIENTS — 4 SERVINGS

8 SERVINGS	INGREDIENTS	4 SERVINGS
2 10-oz. pkgs.	frozen chopped spinach or chopped broccoli	1 10-oz. pkg.
2 10³/₄-oz. cans	reduced-fat and reduced-sodium condensed cream of celery soup	1 10³/₄-oz. can
2 cups	water	1 cup
¹/₄ cup	butter or margarine	2 Tbsp.
6 cups	herb-seasoned stuffing mix	3 cups
4 cups	chopped cooked turkey or chicken	2 cups
²/₃ cup	milk	¹/₃ cup
2 Tbsp.	grated Parmesan cheese	1 Tbsp.

1 In a Dutch oven or large saucepan combine spinach, half of the soup, the water, and butter. Bring to boiling. (If using spinach, separate it with a fork.) Cover and simmer for 5 minutes.

2 Add the stuffing mix to Dutch oven; stir to moisten. Spread mixture in an ungreased 3-quart rectangular baking dish or eight 10-ounce au gratin dishes; top with turkey. Stir milk into remaining soup; pour over turkey. Sprinkle with Parmesan cheese. Bake, uncovered, in a 350° oven about 25 minutes or until heated through.

For 4 servings: Prepare as above, except assemble in a 2-quart square baking dish or four 10-ounce au gratin dishes.

To tote: Cover casserole tightly. Transport in an insulated carrier.

NUTRITION FACTS PER SERVING: 375 cal., 12 g total fat (5 g sat. fat), 65 mg chol., 1,065 mg sodium, 44 g carbo., 5 g fiber, 23 g pro.
DAILY VALUES: 110% vit. A, 18% vit. C, 17% calcium, 23% iron

Chicken and Wild Rice Casserole

For potluck dinners, let guests serve themselves out of the baking dish. For a more special presentation at home, spoon hot portions of the casserole into steamed fresh sweet pepper halves.

PREP: 35 minutes
BAKE: 35 minutes   OVEN: 350°F

INGREDIENTS

16 SERVINGS		8 SERVINGS
2 6-oz. pkgs.	long grain and wild rice mix	1 6-oz. pkg.
6 cups	chopped cooked chicken	3 cups
2 14¹/₂-oz. cans	French-cut green beans, drained	1 14¹/₂-oz. can
2 10³/₄-oz. cans	condensed cream of celery soup	1 10³/₄-oz. can
2 8-oz. cans	sliced water chestnuts, drained	1 8-oz. can
1 cup	mayonnaise or salad dressing	¹/₂ cup
1 cup	chopped onion	¹/₂ cup
¹/₃ cup	sliced almonds	3 Tbsp.
1 4-oz. jar	sliced pimientos, drained	1 2-oz. jar
2 tsp.	lemon juice	1 tsp.
2 cups (8 oz.)	shredded cheddar cheese	1 cup (4 oz.)

1 Prepare rice according to package directions. Meanwhile, in a very large bowl combine chicken, green beans, celery soup, water chestnuts, mayonnaise, onion, almonds, pimientos, and lemon juice. Stir in cooked rice. Divide mixture between two 3-quart rectangular baking dishes.

2 Bake, covered, in a 350° oven for 30 minutes. Uncover and sprinkle with cheese. Bake about 5 minutes more or until casserole is heated through and cheese is melted.

For 8 servings: Prepare as above, except spoon mixture into one 3-quart rectangular baking dish.

Make-ahead directions: Prepare as directed. Cover and chill for up to 24 hours. Bake casserole, covered, in a 350°F oven for 45 minutes. Uncover and sprinkle with cheese. Bake about 5 minutes more or until casserole is heated through and cheese is melted.

To tote: Cover casserole tightly. Transport in an insulated carrier.

NUTRITION FACTS PER SERVING: 406 cal., 23 g total fat (6 g sat. fat), 75 mg chol., 1,048 mg sodium, 25 g carbo., 2 g fiber, 24 g pro.
DAILY VALUES: 12% vit. A, 15% vit. C, 14% calcium, 12% iron

Tomato-Mushroom Chicken Potpie

Who can resist potpie, the ultimate in comfort food? Dried tomatoes update the flavors of a classic favorite.

1 Prepare Potpie Pastry; set aside. In a 12-inch skillet cook onions in hot butter for 2 minutes. Add mushrooms; cook for 3 to 4 minutes more. Stir in flour, oregano, and pepper. Add broth. Cook and stir until bubbly. Add chicken and tomatoes; heat through. Transfer to a 3-quart casserole.

2 On a lightly floured surface, roll pastry to a 12×15-inch rectangle. If desired, use small cutters to cut shapes in pastry, or use a fork to prick pastry. Arrange pastry on top of chicken mixture; trim to ¹/₂ inch beyond rim. Turn under and flute edges. Brush with milk. If desired, top with cutouts. Sprinkle with Parmesan cheese.

3 Place baking dish on a baking sheet. Bake, uncovered, in a 425° oven about 25 minutes or until golden. Let stand for 15 minutes before serving (if toting, see below).

Potpie Pastry: In a bowl stir together 2 cups all-purpose flour, 2 tablespoons cornmeal, 2 tablespoons grated Parmesan cheese, and ¹/₂ teaspoon salt. Cut in ²/₃ cup shortening until pieces are pea size. Sprinkle 1 tablespoon cold water over part of mixture; gently toss with a fork. Push to side of bowl. Repeat with 5 to 7 tablespoons more cold water until all is moistened. Form into a ball.

For 6 servings: Prepare as above, except prepare filling in a large skillet. Transfer chicken mixture to a 1¹/₂-quart casserole. Use half of the ingredients to prepare pastry; roll pastry to a 9-inch circle.

To tote: Do not let stand after baking. Cover tightly. Transport in an insulated carrier.

NUTRITION FACTS PER SERVING: 371 cal., 22 g total fat (7 g sat. fat), 53 mg chol., 435 mg sodium, 25 g carbo., 2 g fiber, 20 g pro.
DAILY VALUES: 5% vit. A, 20% vit. C, 5% calcium, 14% iron

PREP: 45 minutes   BAKE: 25 minutes
STAND: 15 minutes   OVEN: 425°F

INGREDIENTS

12 SERVINGS		6 SERVINGS
1 recipe	Potpie Pastry	¹/₂ recipe
2 cups	chopped onions	1 cup
¹/₄ cup	butter or margarine	2 Tbsp.
6 cups	sliced fresh mushrooms	3 cups
¹/₂ cup	all-purpose flour	¹/₄ cup
1 tsp.	dried oregano, crushed	¹/₂ tsp.
¹/₂ tsp.	black pepper	¹/₄ tsp.
2²/₃ cups	chicken broth	2¹/₂ cups
4 cups	chopped cooked chicken	2 cups
1 14¹/₂-oz. can	diced tomatoes, drained	¹/₂ 14¹/₂-oz. can
²/₃ cup	sliced oil-packed dried tomatoes, drained	¹/₃ cup
2 tsp.	milk	¹/₄ tsp.
2 Tbsp.	grated Parmesan cheese	1 Tbsp.

Chicken Chow Mein Casserole

This family favorite travels well to potlucks. For a lower sodium version use reduced-sodium condensed chicken soup.

PREP: 25 minutes
BAKE: 50 minutes   OVEN: 350°F

1. In a very large bowl stir together chicken, celery, carrots, sweet pepper, mushrooms, almonds, and pimiento. Add soup to chicken mixture; mix well.

2. Transfer chicken mixture to a 3-quart rectangular baking dish. Bake, covered, in a 350° oven for 45 minutes. Uncover; top with chow mein noodles. Bake, uncovered, for 5 to 10 minutes more or until heated through.

For 4 servings: Prepare as above, except transfer chicken mixture to a 2-quart square baking dish. Bake for 30 minutes before topping with chow mein noodles.

To tote: Cover baking dish tightly. Transport in an insulated carrier.

NUTRITION FACTS PER SERVING: 366 cal., 19 g total fat (4 g sat. fat), 68 mg chol., 921 mg sodium, 21 g carbo., 4 g fiber, 27 g pro.
DAILY VALUES: 82% vit. A, 33% vit. C, 8% calcium, 15% iron

8 SERVINGS	INGREDIENTS	4 SERVINGS
4 cups	chopped cooked chicken	2 cups
2 cups	chopped celery	1 cup
1 cup	shredded carrots	1/2 cup
1 cup	chopped green sweet pepper	1/2 cup
2 4-oz. cans	sliced mushrooms, drained	1 4-oz. can
2/3 cup	sliced or slivered almonds, toasted	1/3 cup
2 Tbsp.	diced pimiento, drained	1 Tbsp.
2 10³/4-oz. cans	condensed cream of chicken soup	1 10³/4-oz. can
2 cups	chow mein noodles	1 cup

Baked Chicken Marsala

To tote to a party, simply leave the cheeses and green onions off during the baking time. Place them in a plastic bag. When you reach your destination, sprinkle the chicken with the mixture and rewarm in the oven just until cheese melts.

PREP: 30 minutes
BAKE: 20 minutes   OVEN: 375°F

8 SERVINGS	INGREDIENTS	4 SERVINGS
8 medium	skinless, boneless chicken breast halves	4 medium
1/3 cup	all-purpose flour	3 Tbsp.
6 Tbsp.	butter or margarine	3 Tbsp.
2 cups	sliced fresh mushrooms	1 cup
1 cup	dry Marsala	1/2 cup
2/3 cup	chicken broth	1/3 cup
1/8 tsp.	salt	Dash
1/8 tsp.	black pepper	Dash
1 cup (4 oz.)	shredded mozzarella or fontina cheese	1/2 cup (2 oz.)
2/3 cup	grated Parmesan cheese	1/3 cup
1/2 cup	thinly sliced green onions	1/4 cup

1 Cut each breast half in half lengthwise. Place each chicken piece between 2 pieces of plastic wrap. Using the flat side of a meat mallet, pound each piece to 1/8 inch thick. Remove plastic wrap. Coat chicken lightly with flour.

2 In a 12-inch skillet melt one-third of the butter over medium heat. Add four of the chicken pieces. Cook for 2 minutes on each side. Transfer to a 3-quart rectangular baking dish. Repeat with another one-third of the butter and chicken pieces.

3 Melt the remaining one-third of the butter in the skillet; add mushrooms. Cook and stir until tender; stir in Marsala, broth, salt, and pepper. Bring to boiling; boil gently about 5 minutes or until mixture is reduced to 1 cup (including the mushrooms). Pour over the chicken.

4 Combine mozzarella cheese, Parmesan cheese, and green onions; sprinkle over the chicken. Bake, uncovered, in a 375° oven about 20 minutes or until chicken is no longer pink (170°).

For 4 servings: Prepare as above, except assemble in a 2-quart rectangular baking dish and cook mushroom mixture until reduced to 1/2 cup.

To tote: Cover baking dish tightly. Transport in an insulated carrier.

NUTRITION FACTS PER SERVING: 364 cal., 17 g total fat (9 g sat. fat), 121 mg chol., 496 mg sodium, 6 g carbo., 0 g fiber, 42 g pro.
DAILY VALUES: 11% vit. A, 4% vit. C, 23% calcium, 9% iron

Cajun Chicken Lasagna

Tired of plain lasagna? This version, spiced up with Cajun seasoning and andouille sausage, will surely become a perennial favorite.

1 Cook lasagna noodles according to package directions. Drain noodles; rinse with cold water. Drain well.

2 Meanwhile, in a bowl combine sausage, chicken, Cajun seasoning, and sage. In a large skillet cook and stir chicken mixture about 8 minutes or until chicken is no longer pink. Using a slotted spoon, remove chicken mixture from skillet, reserving drippings in skillet. Set chicken mixture aside. In the same skillet cook onion, celery, sweet pepper, and garlic in drippings until vegetables are tender. Return chicken mixture to skillet; stir in half of the Alfredo sauce and the Parmesan cheese.

3 Lightly coat a 3-quart rectangular baking dish with cooking spray. Place one-fourth of the noodles in the bottom of the dish, cutting as necessary to fit. Spread with one-third of the chicken-vegetable mixture. Sprinkle with one-third of the mozzarella cheese. Repeat layers twice; top with remaining noodles. Carefully spread remaining Alfredo sauce over the top.

4 Bake, covered, in a 350° oven about 1 hour or until heated through. Let stand for 15 to 20 minutes before serving.

For 6 servings: Prepare as above, except assemble in a 2-quart square baking dish and bake for 30 to 35 minutes or until heated through.

To tote: Do not let stand after baking. Cover tightly. Transport in an insulated carrier.

NUTRITION FACTS PER SERVING: 507 cal., 31 g total fat (7 g sat. fat), 83 mg chol., 938 mg sodium, 27 g carbo., 1 g fiber, 29 g pro.
DAILY VALUES: 3% vit. A, 8% vit. C, 18% calcium, 10% iron

PREP: 45 minutes BAKE: 1 hour
STAND: 15 minutes OVEN: 350°F

12 SERVINGS	INGREDIENTS	6 SERVINGS
16	dried lasagna noodles	8
1 lb.	cooked andouille sausage or smoked pork sausage, quartered lengthwise and sliced	8 oz.
1 lb.	skinless, boneless chicken breast halves, cut into 3/4-inch pieces	8 oz.
2 to 3 tsp.	Cajun seasoning	1 to 1 1/2 tsp.
1 tsp.	dried sage, crushed	1/2 tsp.
1/2 cup	chopped onion	1/4 cup
1/2 cup	chopped celery	1/4 cup
1/4 cup	chopped green sweet pepper	2 Tbsp.
6 cloves	garlic, minced	3 cloves
2 10-oz. containers	refrigerated Alfredo sauce	1 10-oz. container
1/2 cup	grated Parmesan cheese	1/4 cup
	Nonstick cooking spray	
2 1/2 cups (6 oz.)	shredded mozzarella cheese	3/4 cup (3 oz.)

Creamy Chicken-Broccoli Bake

Tried-and-true chicken and broccoli bake is a must for most potluck gatherings. Be sure to take enough!

PREP: 30 minutes
BAKE: 55 minutes OVEN: 350°F

12 SERVINGS — INGREDIENTS — 6 SERVINGS

12 SERVINGS	INGREDIENTS	6 SERVINGS
	Nonstick cooking spray	
10 oz.	dried medium noodles	6 oz.
1$^1/_2$ lb.	skinless, boneless chicken breast halves, cut into bite-size pieces	12 oz.
3 cups	sliced fresh mushrooms	1$^1/_2$ cups
8	green onions, sliced	4
1 medium	red sweet pepper, chopped	$^1/_2$ medium
2 10$^3/_4$-oz. cans	condensed cream of broccoli soup	1 10$^3/_4$-oz. can
2 8-oz. cartons	dairy sour cream	1 8-oz. carton
$^1/_3$ cup	chicken broth	$^1/_4$ cup
2 tsp.	dry mustard	1 tsp.
$^1/_4$ tsp.	black pepper	$^1/_8$ tsp.
1 16-oz. pkg.	frozen chopped broccoli, thawed and drained	1 10-oz. pkg.
$^1/_2$ cup	fine dry bread crumbs	$^1/_4$ cup
2 Tbsp.	butter or margarine, melted	1 Tbsp.

1 Coat a 3-quart rectangular baking dish with cooking spray; set dish aside.

2 Cook noodles according to package directions; drain. Rinse with cold water; drain again.

3 Meanwhile, coat a large skillet with cooking spray. Heat over medium heat. Add chicken to skillet. Cook and stir about 3 minutes or until chicken is no longer pink. Transfer chicken from the skillet to a large bowl.

4 Add mushrooms, green onions, and sweet pepper to skillet. Cook and stir until vegetables are tender. (If necessary, add 1 tablespoon cooking oil to skillet.)

5 Transfer vegetables to bowl with chicken. Stir in soup, sour cream, broth, mustard, and black pepper. Gently stir in cooked noodles and broccoli.

6 Spoon chicken mixture into prepared baking dish. Mix bread crumbs and melted butter; sprinkle over chicken mixture. Bake, covered, in a 350° oven for 30 minutes. Uncover and bake about 25 minutes more or until heated through.

For 6 servings: Prepare as above, except assemble in a 2-quart square baking dish. Bake, covered, for 30 minutes. Uncover and bake about 15 minutes more or until heated through.

To tote: Cover baking dish tightly. Transport in an insulated carrier.

NUTRITION FACTS PER SERVING: 336 cal., 15 g total fat (8 g sat. fat), 79 mg chol., 515 mg sodium, 29 g carbo., 3 g fiber, 21 g pro.
DAILY VALUES: 35% vit. A, 63% vit. C, 10% calcium, 12% iron

Creamy Chicken Enchiladas

This enchilada dish will be the hit of the party. Chicken and spinach create the tasty filling, while sour cream is the basis for the sauce.

**PREP: 40 minutes BAKE: 40 minutes
STAND: 5 minutes OVEN: 350°F**

12 SERVINGS	INGREDIENTS	6 SERVINGS
1 lb.	skinless, boneless chicken breast halves	8 oz.
1 10-oz. pkg.	frozen chopped spinach, thawed and well drained	1/2 10-oz. pkg.
1/2 cup	thinly sliced green onions	1/4 cup
2 8-oz. cartons	light dairy sour cream	1 8-oz. carton
1/2 cup	plain yogurt	1/4 cup
1/4 cup	all-purpose flour	2 Tbsp.
1/2 tsp.	ground cumin	1/4 tsp.
1/2 tsp.	salt	1/4 tsp.
1 cup	milk	1/2 cup
2 4-oz. cans	diced green chile peppers, drained	1 4-oz. can
12 7-inch	flour tortillas	6 7-inch
2/3 cup	shredded cheddar or Monterey Jack cheese	1/3 cup
	Salsa (optional)	
	Sliced green onions (optional)	

1 In a large saucepan place chicken in enough water to cover. Bring to boiling; reduce heat. Simmer, covered, for 12 to 14 minutes or until chicken is no longer pink (170°). Drain well. When cool enough to handle, use a fork to shred chicken into bite-size pieces.

2 Combine shredded chicken, spinach, and green onions; set aside. For sauce, stir together sour cream, yogurt, flour, cumin, and salt. Stir in milk and chile peppers. Divide sauce in half.

3 For filling, combine one half of the sauce and the chicken-spinach mixture; divide mixture into 12 portions. Place a portion of filling near one end of a tortilla; roll up. Place filled tortilla, seam side down, in an ungreased 3-quart rectangular baking dish. Repeat with remaining tortillas and filling.

4 Spoon remaining sauce over tortillas. Bake, uncovered, in a 350° oven about 40 minutes or until heated through. Remove from oven; sprinkle with cheese. Let stand for 5 minutes before serving. If desired, serve with salsa and additional green onions.

For 6 enchiladas: Prepare as above, except place enchiladas in an ungreased 2-quart square baking dish.

To tote: Cover tightly after sprinkling with cheese. Transport in an insulated carrier. If desired, transport salsa and green onions in an insulated cooler with ice packs.

NUTRITION FACTS PER ENCHILADA: 247 cal., 9 g total fat (4 g sat. fat), 44 mg chol., 395 mg sodium, 23 g carbo., 1 g fiber, 18 g pro.
DAILY VALUES: 43% vit. A, 18% vit. C, 26% calcium, 11% iron

Spinach-Sauced Chicken Breast Halves

For a more finished presentation at home, toss hot spaghetti with a little butter and olive oil, and serve the chicken on a bed of the spaghetti.

1 In a shallow dish combine bread crumbs and Parmesan cheese. Coat chicken breast halves with crumb mixture. Arrange chicken in a 3-quart rectangular baking dish. Set remaining crumb mixture aside.

2 In a saucepan cook green onions in hot butter until tender. Stir in flour. Stir in milk all at once. Cook and stir until thickened and bubbly. Stir in spinach and ham.

3 Spoon spinach mixture over chicken; sprinkle with remaining crumb mixture. Bake, uncovered, in a 350° oven for 40 to 45 minutes or until chicken is no longer pink (170°).

For 6 servings: Prepare as above, except arrange chicken in a 2-quart rectangular baking dish.

To tote: Cover baking dish tightly. Transport in an insulated carrier.

NUTRITION FACTS PER SERVING: 234 cal., 6 g total fat (3 g sat. fat), 90 mg chol., 468 mg sodium, 8 g carbo., 1 g fiber, 36 g pro.
DAILY VALUES: 40% vit. A, 13% vit. C, 11% calcium, 9% iron

PREP: 20 minutes
BAKE: 40 minutes   OVEN: 350°F

12 SERVINGS	INGREDIENTS	6 SERVINGS
3/4 cup	Italian-seasoned fine dry bread crumbs	1/3 cup
1/4 cup	grated Parmesan cheese	2 Tbsp.
12	skinless, boneless chicken breast halves	6
1/2 cup	sliced green onions	1/4 cup
2 Tbsp.	butter or margarine	1 Tbsp.
2 Tbsp.	all-purpose flour	1 Tbsp.
1 cup	milk	1/2 cup
1 10-oz. pkg.	frozen chopped spinach, thawed and well drained	1/2 10-oz. pkg.
1 4-oz. pkg.	boiled ham slices, diced	1/2 4-oz. pkg.

Spinach-Stuffed Chicken Rolls

Serve this chicken warm or cold. Either way it's an impressive dish to take to your next potluck or party.

1 For filling, in a large skillet cook onion, mushrooms, and garlic in the 2 tablespoons hot butter until tender. Stir in spinach, oregano, salt, and pepper; set filling aside.

2 Place each chicken breast half between two pieces of plastic wrap. Using the flat side of a meat mallet, pound each chicken breast lightly into a rectangle about 1/8 inch thick. Remove plastic wrap.

3 Divide the filling evenly among the chicken breast halves. Fold in sides; roll up. If necessary, secure with wooden toothpicks.

4 In a shallow dish combine bread crumbs, Parmesan cheese, and paprika. In another shallow dish combine beaten egg and water. Dip chicken rolls in the egg mixture; coat with bread crumb mixture. Place rolls, seam side down, in a lightly greased 3-quart rectangular baking dish. Drizzle with the 3 tablespoons melted butter.

5 Bake, uncovered, in a 350° oven for 20 to 25 minutes or until chicken is no longer pink (170°).

For 4 servings: Prepare as above, except place chicken rolls in a 2-quart rectangular baking dish.

To tote: Cover dish tightly. Transport in an insulated carrier.

NUTRITION FACTS PER SERVING: 287 cal., 11 g total fat (6 g sat. fat), 105 mg chol., 569 mg sodium, 8 g carbo., 2 g fiber, 37 g pro.
DAILY VALUES: 61% vit. A, 13% vit. C, 12% calcium, 12% iron

PREP: 40 minutes
BAKE: 20 minutes OVEN: 350°F

8 SERVINGS	INGREDIENTS	4 SERVINGS
2/3 cup	chopped onion	1/3 cup
2/3 cup	chopped fresh mushrooms	1/3 cup
2 cloves	garlic, minced	1 clove
2 Tbsp.	butter or margarine	1 Tbsp.
1 10-oz. pkg.	frozen chopped spinach, thawed and well drained	1/2 10-oz. pkg.
3/4 tsp.	dried oregano, crushed	1/2 tsp.
1/2 tsp.	salt	1/4 tsp.
1/4 tsp.	black pepper	Dash
8 medium	skinless, boneless chicken breast halves	4 medium
2/3 cup	fine dry bread crumbs	1/3 cup
1/4 cup	grated Parmesan cheese	2 Tbsp.
1/2 tsp.	paprika	1/4 tsp.
2	slightly beaten egg(s)	1
1 Tbsp.	water	1 Tbsp.
3 Tbsp.	butter or margarine, melted	4 1/2 tsp.

Chile Relleños Chicken

In this recipe, classic cheese-stuffed chile pepper is rolled up in chicken. Serve along with Spanish-style rice and refried beans for a Mexican-inspired meal.

PREP: 25 minutes
BAKE: 40 minutes   OVEN: 375°F

INGREDIENTS

8 SERVINGS		4 SERVINGS
8 medium	skinless, boneless chicken breast halves	4 medium
1 cup (4 oz.)	shredded taco cheese or cheddar cheese	1/2 cup (2 oz.)
1/4 cup	finely chopped onion	2 Tbsp.
1/4 cup	snipped fresh cilantro (optional)	2 Tbsp.
2 tsp.	chili powder	1 tsp.
8	canned whole green chile peppers, drained	4
2	beaten egg(s)	1
2 Tbsp.	milk	1 Tbsp.
1/2 cup	fine dry bread crumbs	1/4 cup
1 tsp.	salt	1/2 tsp.

1 Place each chicken breast half between two pieces of plastic wrap. Using the flat side of a meat mallet, pound each chicken breast lightly to about 1/4 inch thick. Remove plastic wrap. Set chicken aside.

2 In a small bowl combine the cheese, onion, cilantro (if desired), and half of the chili powder. Stuff some of the cheese mixture into each whole chile pepper.

3 Place a stuffed pepper on top of each flattened chicken breast. Roll up chicken around pepper, folding in sides. If necessary, secure chicken with wooden toothpicks.

4 In a shallow dish combine the eggs and milk. In another shallow dish stir together the bread crumbs, the remaining chili powder, and salt. Dip chicken rolls in egg mixture; coat with bread crumb mixture.

5 Place chicken rolls in an ungreased 3-quart rectangular baking dish. Bake, uncovered, in a 375° oven about 40 minutes or until chicken is no longer pink (170°).

For 4 servings: Prepare as above, except bake chicken in a 2-quart square baking dish.

Make-ahead directions: Prepare as directed. Cover and chill for up to 2 hours. Bake as directed.

To tote: Cover baking dish tightly. Transport in an insulated carrier.

NUTRITION FACTS PER SERVING: 266 cal., 4 g total fat (4 g sat. fat), 149 mg chol., 720 mg sodium, 6 g carbo., 1 g fiber, 36 g pro.
DAILY VALUES: 15% vit. A, 19% vit. C, 17% calcium, 10% iron

Vegetable Chicken Lasagna

Don't be surprised if this cheesy, yet healthful lasagna becomes your family's favorite recipe. It's full of rich nutrients from the spinach, tomatoes, and carrots, and best of all—it's lower in fat and calories than traditional lasagna.

1 For cheese filling, in a small bowl combine ricotta cheese, spinach, egg, and half of the Italian seasoning. Cover; chill until ready to assemble lasagna.

2 For sauce, in a large skillet cook chicken, mushrooms, onion, and remaining Italian seasoning in hot oil for 4 to 5 minutes or until chicken is no longer pink. Stir in tomatoes, tomato sauce, carrots, and pepper. Bring to boiling; reduce heat. Simmer, uncovered, about 15 minutes or until mixture is slightly thickened, stirring occasionally.

3 Meanwhile, cook lasagna noodles according to package directions. Drain noodles; rinse with cold water. Drain well.

4 Lightly coat a 3-quart rectangular baking dish with cooking spray. Place one-third of the lasagna noodles in prepared dish. Spread half of the cheese mixture over the noodles. Spread one-third of the sauce over cheese mixture. Sprinkle with one-fourth of the mozzarella cheese. Repeat layers, ending with noodles. Spoon remaining sauce over top. Sprinkle with remaining mozzarella cheese.

5 Bake, covered, in a 350° oven for 35 minutes. Uncover and bake for 5 to 10 minutes more or until cheese is bubbly. Let stand 10 minutes before serving.

For 4 servings: Prepare as above, except use 1 egg yolk rather than a whole egg.* Assemble in a 2-quart rectangular baking dish, using 2 noodles per layer (cut noodles as necessary to fit).

To tote: Do not let stand after baking. Cover tightly. Transport in an insulated carrier.

NUTRITION FACTS PER SERVING: 400 cal., 16 g total fat (8 g sat. fat), 102 mg chol., 552 mg sodium, 31 g carbo., 4 g fiber, 33 g pro.
DAILY VALUES: 218% vit. A, 41% vit. C, 40% calcium, 18% iron

PREP: 45 minutes BAKE: 40 minutes
STAND: 10 minutes OVEN: 350°F

8 SERVINGS	INGREDIENTS	4 SERVINGS
1 15-oz. carton	ricotta cheese	1 cup
1 10-oz. pkg.	frozen chopped spinach, thawed and well drained	1/2 10-oz. pkg.
1	slightly beaten egg (or yolk)	1*
2 tsp.	dried Italian seasoning, crushed	1 tsp.
1 lb.	skinless, boneless chicken breast halves, cut into 1/2-inch pieces	8 oz.
3 cups	sliced fresh mushrooms	1 1/2 cups
1/2 cup	chopped onion	1/4 cup
1 Tbsp.	olive oil	1 1/2 tsp.
2 14 1/2-oz. cans	diced tomatoes, undrained	1 14 1/2-oz. can
1 8-oz. can	tomato sauce	1/2 cup
2 cups	shredded carrots	1 cup
1/2 tsp.	black pepper	1/4 tsp.
9	dried lasagna noodles	6
	Nonstick cooking spray	
2 cups (8 oz.)	shredded mozzarella cheese	1 cup (4 oz.)

Sweet-and-Sour Baked Chicken

Baking makes classic sweet-and-sour chicken easier to make—and more totable. For a family-size version, serve this with hot cooked rice.

PREP: 25 minutes
BAKE: 30 minutes OVEN: 350°F

8 SERVINGS	INGREDIENTS	4 SERVINGS
8 medium	skinless, boneless chicken breast halves	4 medium
	Salt and black pepper	
2 Tbsp.	cooking oil	1 Tbsp.
1 20-oz. can	pineapple chunks (juice pack)	1 8-oz. can
1 cup	jellied cranberry sauce	1/2 cup
1/4 cup	cornstarch	2 Tbsp.
1/4 cup	packed brown sugar	2 Tbsp.
1/4 cup	rice vinegar or cider vinegar	2 Tbsp.
1/4 cup	frozen orange juice concentrate, thawed	2 Tbsp.
1/4 cup	dry sherry, chicken broth, or water	2 Tbsp.
1/4 cup	soy sauce	2 Tbsp.
1/2 tsp.	ground ginger	1/4 tsp.
2 medium	green sweet pepper(s), cut into bite-size strips	1 medium

1 Sprinkle chicken lightly with salt and pepper. Heat oil in a large skillet over medium-high heat. Add chicken and cook about 2 minutes on each side or until brown. (If necessary, brown chicken in batches.) Transfer chicken to a 3-quart rectangular baking dish. Drain pineapple well, reserving 2/3 cup juice. Spoon pineapple chunks evenly over chicken in dish; set aside.

2 For sauce, in a medium saucepan whisk together the reserved pineapple juice, the cranberry sauce, cornstarch, brown sugar, vinegar, orange juice concentrate, sherry, soy sauce, and ginger. Cook and stir over medium heat until thickened and bubbly. Pour over chicken and pineapple in dish.

3 Bake, covered, in a 350° oven for 25 minutes. Uncover and add sweet pepper strips, stirring gently to coat with sauce. Bake, uncovered, about 5 minutes more or until chicken is no longer pink (170°).

For 4 servings: Prepare as above, except reserve only 1/3 cup pineapple juice. Transfer browned chicken to a 2-quart square baking dish.

To tote: Cover dish tightly. Transport in an insulated carrier.

NUTRITION FACTS PER SERVING: 368 cal., 6 g total fat (1 g sat. fat), 82 mg chol., 589 mg sodium, 41 g carbo., 2 g fiber, 35 g pro.
DAILY VALUES: 5% vit. A, 73% vit. C, 4% calcium, 9% iron

Crunchy Chicken Fingers

Every bite is moist and juicy. Coated in sour cream and herbed stuffing mix, the chicken has lots of flavor. Finger shapes make a fun presentation.

PREP: 20 minutes
BAKE: 25 minutes   OVEN: 375°F

10 SERVINGS	INGREDIENTS	6 SERVINGS
8 medium	skinless, boneless chicken breast halves	4 medium
1 8-oz. carton	dairy sour cream	1/2 cup
2 Tbsp.	lemon juice	1 Tbsp.
1 Tbsp.	Worcestershire sauce	1 1/2 tsp.
1 tsp.	paprika	1/2 tsp.
1/4 tsp.	celery salt	1/8 tsp.
1/4 tsp.	black pepper	1/8 tsp.
1 8-oz. pkg. (4 cups)	herb-seasoned stuffing mix, coarsely crushed	1/2 8-oz. pkg. (2 cups)
1/4 cup	butter or margarine, melted	2 Tbsp.

1 Cut chicken into 3/4-inch strips; set aside. In a shallow bowl combine sour cream, lemon juice, Worcestershire sauce, paprika, celery salt, and black pepper.

2 Dip chicken strips into sour cream mixture; coat with crushed stuffing mix. Arrange chicken strips in two large shallow baking pans (pieces shouldn't touch). Drizzle melted butter over chicken.

3 Bake, uncovered, in a 375° oven about 25 minutes or until chicken is no longer pink, rotating pans after 15 minutes.

For 6 servings: Prepare as above, except arrange chicken strips in one large shallow baking pan.

To tote: Cover chicken tightly. Transport in an insulated carrier.

NUTRITION FACTS PER SERVING: 312 cal., 12 g total fat (6 g sat. fat), 89 mg chol., 496 mg sodium, 19 g carbo., 2 g fiber, 30 g pro.
DAILY VALUES: 10% vit. A, 5% vit. C, 7% calcium, 10% iron

Red Chicken Enchiladas

Shredded chicken, which is simmered in onion, cilantro, and spices, makes up the filling for these party-worthy enchiladas.

PREP: 1 hour BAKE: 20 minutes
STAND: 5 minutes OVEN: 350°F

INGREDIENTS

10 SERVINGS		5 SERVINGS
1¹/₂ lb.	skinless, boneless chicken breast halves	12 oz.
1 cup	chopped onion	¹/₂ cup
¹/₂ cup	loosely packed fresh cilantro	¹/₄ cup
1 tsp.	crushed red pepper	¹/₂ tsp.
2	fresh jalapeño chile pepper(s), seeded and chopped	1
2 tsp.	chili powder	1 tsp.
1 clove	garlic, minced	1 small clove
1 Tbsp.	cooking oil	1¹/₂ tsp.
1 19-oz. can	enchilada sauce	¹/₂ 19-oz. can (about 1 cup)
10 6-inch	corn tortillas	5 6-inch
1 cup (4 oz.)	shredded Monterey Jack or cheddar cheese	¹/₂ cup (2 oz.)
¹/₂ cup	sliced pitted ripe olives	¹/₄ cup
	Dairy sour cream (optional)	
3	green onions, thinly sliced (optional)	2

1 In a large saucepan combine chicken, half of the onion, the cilantro, half of the crushed red pepper, half of the chopped jalapeño peppers, the chili powder, and garlic. Add enough water to cover chicken. Bring to boiling; reduce heat. Simmer, covered, for 15 to 20 minutes or until chicken is no longer pink (170°). Drain well. When cool enough to handle, use a fork to shred chicken into bite-size pieces.

2 In a large skillet heat oil over medium-high heat. Add remaining onion, crushed red pepper, and jalapeño peppers. Reduce heat; cook and stir over low heat about 2 minutes or until onion is tender. Add chicken and ¹/₂ cup of the enchilada sauce to skillet. Bring to boiling; reduce heat. Simmer, covered, for 10 minutes, stirring occasionally.

3 Spoon ¹/₃ cup of chicken mixture onto each tortilla near one edge; roll up. Place enchiladas, seam sides down, in a lightly greased 2-quart rectangular baking dish. Pour remaining sauce over all. Bake, covered, in a 350° oven for 20 to 25 minutes. Uncover; sprinkle with cheese. Let stand for 5 minutes. Sprinkle with olives and, if desired, top with sour cream and green onions.

For 5 enchiladas: Prepare as above, except use a medium saucepan to cook chicken. Use a small saucepan to cook onion mixture. Place in a 2-quart square baking dish; bake for 15 to 20 minutes.

To tote: Cover tightly after sprinkling with cheese. Transport in an insulated carrier. Transport olives and, if desired, green onions and sour cream in an insulated cooler with ice packs.

NUTRITION FACTS PER ENCHILADA: 234 cal., 8 g total fat (3 g sat. fat), 49 mg chol., 519 mg sodium, 19 g carbo., 3 g fiber, 21 g pro.
DAILY VALUES: 15% vit. A, 10% vit. C, 14% calcium, 15% iron

Glazed Cranberry Chicken

Four-ingredient recipes are all the rage. But what about their flavor? This one is sure to please your party guests.

If desired, skin chicken. Arrange chicken pieces in two 3-quart rectangular baking dishes. For glaze, in a bowl combine cranberry sauce, salad dressing, and soup mix. Pour glaze over chicken in both baking dishes.

Bake, uncovered, in a 350° oven about 1 hour or until the chicken is no longer pink (170° for breasts, 180° for thighs and drumsticks). Stir glaze and spoon over chicken once or twice during baking. Serve chicken and glaze on a platter. If desired, serve with hot cooked rice.

For 4 servings: Prepare as above, except arrange chicken in one 3-quart rectangular baking dish.

Make-ahead directions: Cover and chill chicken for 8 hours or overnight before baking. Bake as directed in step 2.

To tote: Cover chicken tightly. Transport chicken and, if desired, rice in an insulated carrier. Just before serving, transfer chicken and glaze to a serving platter.

NUTRITION FACTS PER SERVING: 581 cal., 18 g total fat (5 g sat. fat), 133 mg chol., 880 mg sodium, 62 g carbo., 1 g fiber, 42 g pro.
DAILY VALUES: 1% vit. A, 9% vit. C, 3% calcium, 13% iron

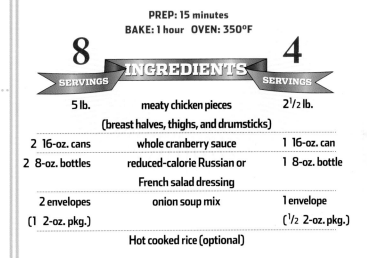

PREP: 15 minutes
BAKE: 1 hour   OVEN: 350°F

8 SERVINGS — INGREDIENTS — **4 SERVINGS**

8 SERVINGS	INGREDIENTS	4 SERVINGS
5 lb.	meaty chicken pieces (breast halves, thighs, and drumsticks)	2½ lb.
2 16-oz. cans	whole cranberry sauce	1 16-oz. can
2 8-oz. bottles	reduced-calorie Russian or French salad dressing	1 8-oz. bottle
2 envelopes (1 2-oz. pkg.)	onion soup mix	1 envelope (½ 2-oz. pkg.)
	Hot cooked rice (optional)	

Taco Pasta

Hungry for Mexican food? This combination of pasta, salsa, ground chicken, and cheese will satisfy your craving.

PREP: 20 minutes
BAKE: 45 minutes OVEN: 350°F

12 SERVINGS	INGREDIENTS	6 SERVINGS
8 oz.	dried penne	4 oz.
2 lb.	uncooked ground chicken	1 lb.
1 cup	chopped onion	1/2 cup
1 1/2 cups	water	3/4 cup
1 1 1/4-oz. envelope	taco seasoning mix	1/2 1 1/4-oz. envelope
2 11-oz. cans	whole-kernel corn with sweet peppers, drained	1 11-oz. can
2 cups	sliced pitted ripe olives	1 cup
2 cups (8 oz.)	shredded cheddar cheese	1 cup (4 oz.)
1 cup	salsa	1/2 cup
2 4-oz. cans	diced green chile peppers, drained	1 4-oz. can
8 cups	shredded lettuce	4 cups
2 medium	tomato(es), cut into thin wedges	1 medium
	Tortilla chips (optional)	
	Dairy sour cream (optional)	

1 Cook pasta according to package directions; drain and set aside.

2 Meanwhile, in a 12-inch skillet cook ground chicken and onion, half at a time, until meat is brown; drain fat. Return all of the chicken mixture to skillet. Stir in water and taco seasoning mix. Bring to boiling; reduce heat. Simmer, uncovered, for 2 minutes, stirring occasionally. Stir in cooked pasta, corn, olives, half of the shredded cheese, salsa, and chile peppers.

3 Transfer pasta mixture to a lightly greased 3-quart rectangular baking dish. Bake, covered, in a 350° oven for 45 minutes or until heated through. Remove from oven; sprinkle with remaining cheese.

4 Serve with lettuce, tomato wedges, and, if desired, tortilla chips and sour cream.

For 6 servings: Prepare as above, except transfer mixture to a 2-quart rectangular baking dish. Bake for 30 minutes.

To tote: Cover baking dish tightly. Transport in an insulated carrier. Transport lettuce, tomatoes, and, if desired, sour cream in an insulated cooler with ice packs. If desired, transport chips in an airtight bag or container.

NUTRITION FACTS PER SERVING: 351 cal., 17 g total fat (4 g sat. fat), 20 mg chol., 934 mg sodium, 30 g carbo., 4 g fiber, 24 g pro.
DAILY VALUES: 14% vit. A, 31% vit. C, 21% calcium, 17% iron

CHAPTER 3

FAMILY-APPROVED MEAT DISHES

p. 83   p. 89

p. 90   p. 99

p. 109   p. 117

Visit our Recipe Center at www.bhg.com/bkrecipe

Down-South Barbecue
Sandwiches, p.100

Stuffed Cabbage Rolls

These plump cabbage rolls are nestled on a bed of sauerkraut. Not fond of sauerkraut? Just omit the kraut layer in the bottom of the dish.

PREP: 50 minutes
BAKE: 40 minutes OVEN: 350°F

8 SERVINGS | INGREDIENTS | 4 SERVINGS

8 SERVINGS	INGREDIENTS	4 SERVINGS
16 large	cabbage leaves	8 large
1½ lb.	lean ground beef	¾ lb.
1 cup	chopped onion	½ cup
2 cups	cooked white rice	1 cup
2	slightly beaten egg(s)	1
¼ cup	snipped fresh parsley	2 Tbsp.
½ tsp.	salt	¼ tsp.
1 32-oz. jar	sauerkraut, rinsed and well drained	1 14-oz. can
1 15-oz. can	tomato sauce	1 8-oz. can
¼ cup	water	2 Tbsp.
¼ cup	packed brown sugar	2 Tbsp.
4 tsp.	lemon juice	2 tsp.
Dash	ground allspice	Dash

1 Trim veins from cabbage leaves. Immerse leaves, four at a time, into boiling water. Cook for 2 to 3 minutes or just until leaves are limp. Carefully remove leaves with tongs or a slotted spoon; drain well.

2 Meanwhile, for filling, in a large skillet cook ground beef and onion until meat is brown; drain off fat. In a medium bowl combine cooked beef mixture, rice, eggs, parsley, and salt.

3 Lightly grease two 2-quart rectangular or square baking dishes; divide sauerkraut evenly between the two dishes.

4 Place about ⅓ cup of the filling in the center of each cabbage leaf; fold in sides. Starting at an unfolded edge, carefully roll each leaf, making sure folded sides are tucked into the roll. Arrange cabbage rolls on sauerkraut in baking dishes.

5 For sauce, stir together the tomato sauce, water, brown sugar, lemon juice, and allspice; pour sauce over cabbage rolls. Bake, covered, in a 350° oven about 40 minutes or until heated through.

For 4 servings: Prepare as above, except assemble and bake in one 2-quart rectangular baking dish.

To tote: Transport in an insulated carrier.

NUTRITION FACTS PER SERVING: 285 cal., 10 g total fat (4 g sat. fat), 107 mg chol., 1,242 mg sodium, 29 g carbo., 6 g fiber, 19 g pro.
DAILY VALUES: 5% vit. A, 50% vit. C, 5% calcium, 16% iron.

Eggplant and Beef Casserole

Eggplant, ground beef, Italian seasoning, and a combination of mozzarella and Parmesan cheeses join forces in this delicious dinner-in-a-dish.

PREP: 50 minutes BAKE: 30 minutes
STAND: 10 minutes OVEN: 350°F

8 SERVINGS — INGREDIENTS — 6 SERVINGS

8 servings	Ingredients	6 servings
³/₄ cup	milk	¹/₂ cup
1	beaten egg	1
³/₄ cup	all-purpose flour	¹/₂ cup
¹/₂ tsp.	salt	¹/₄ tsp.
¹/₄ tsp.	black pepper	¹/₈ tsp.
1 1¹/₂-lb.	eggplant, peeled and sliced ¹/₂ inch thick	1 1-lb.
3 Tbsp.	cooking oil	2 Tbsp.
1 lb.	lean ground beef	12 oz.
1 cup	chopped green sweet pepper	³/₄ cup
³/₄ cup	chopped onion	¹/₂ cup
1 15-oz. can	tomato sauce	1 15-oz. can
1 8-oz. can	tomato sauce	omit
1¹/₂ tsp.	dried Italian seasoning, crushed	1 tsp.
2 cups (8 oz.)	shredded Italian blend cheeses	1¹/₂ cups (6 oz.)

1 Grease a 3-quart rectangular baking dish; set dish aside. In a small bowl combine milk and egg. In a shallow dish combine flour, salt, and pepper.

2 Dip eggplant slices in egg mixture; coat with flour mixture. In a 12-inch skillet cook eggplant slices, several at a time, in hot oil for 2 minutes on each side or until golden. Repeat with remaining eggplant slices, adding more oil if necessary. Drain on paper towels.

3 In a large skillet cook ground beef, sweet pepper, and onion until meat is brown; drain off fat. Stir in tomato sauce and Italian seasoning.

4 Layer half of the eggplant slices in the prepared baking dish, cutting slices to fit. Spread with half of the meat mixture; sprinkle with half of the cheese. Repeat layers. Bake, covered, in a 350° oven for 20 minutes. Uncover and bake for 10 to 15 minutes more or until heated through. Let stand 10 minutes before serving (if toting, see below).

For 6 servings: Prepare as above, except assemble and bake in a 2-quart rectangular baking dish.

To tote: Do not let stand after baking. Cover tightly. Transport in an insulated carrier.

NUTRITION FACTS PER SERVING: 340 cal., 19 g total fat (7 g sat. fat), 84 mg chol., 796 mg sodium, 23 g carbo., 4 g fiber, 22 g pro.
DAILY VALUES: 5% vit. A, 41% vit. C, 21% calcium, 14% iron

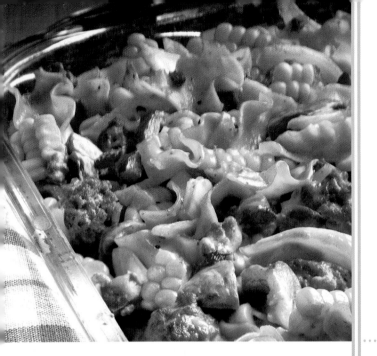

Beefy Vegetables and Noodles

There is more to this casserole than the title suggests. Fresh corn, sweet pepper, pimientos, onion, and mushrooms add interest and vitamins to this creamy dish.

PREP: 35 minutes
BAKE: 30 minutes   OVEN: 350°F

12 SERVINGS	INGREDIENTS	6 SERVINGS
2 8-oz. pkgs.	extra-wide noodles	1 8-oz. pkg.
2 lb.	lean ground beef or ground raw turkey	1 lb.
1½ cups	coarsely chopped green sweet pepper	¾ cup
1 cup	chopped onion	½ cup
1 16-oz. pkg. 4	frozen whole kernel corn, OR fresh ears of corn, cooked and cut off the cob	1 10-oz. pkg. 2
2 10¾-oz. cans	condensed golden mushroom soup	1 10¾-oz. can
2 cups	chopped fresh mushrooms	1 cup
1 8-oz. pkg.	cream cheese, cut up	½ 8-oz. pkg.
⅔ cup	milk	⅓ cup
1 4-oz. jar	diced pimientos, drained	1 2-oz. jar
1 tsp.	salt	½ tsp.
1 tsp.	dried marjoram, crushed	½ tsp.
½ tsp.	black pepper	¼ tsp.

1 Cook noodles according to package directions. Drain; rinse and drain well.

2 Meanwhile, in a 4-quart Dutch oven cook ground beef, sweet pepper, and onion until meat is brown and vegetables are tender; drain off fat. Stir in corn, soup, mushrooms, cream cheese, milk, pimientos, salt, marjoram, and pepper. Heat and stir until cream cheese melts. Gently stir in cooked noodles.

3 Divide ground beef mixture between two ungreased 2-quart rectangular baking dishes. Bake, covered, in a 350° oven for 30 to 35 minutes until heated through.

For 6 servings: Prepare as above, except spoon mixture into one ungreased 2-quart rectangular baking dish.

To tote: Transport in an insulated carrier.

NUTRITION FACTS PER SERVING: 416 cal., 18 g total fat (8 g sat. fat), 107 mg chol., 688 mg sodium, 41 g carbo., 3 g fiber, 23 g pro.
DAILY VALUES: 22% vit. A, 42% vit. C, 5% calcium, 20% iron

Pastitsio

Pastitsio (pah-STEET-see-oh) is a Greek-style pasta casserole with a white sauce. Wow your potluck friends with your talents in cooking ethnic fare.

1 For meat sauce, in a large skillet cook ground beef and onion until meat is brown; drain off fat. Stir in tomato sauce, wine, and cinnamon. Bring to boiling; reduce heat. Simmer, covered, for 30 minutes, stirring occasionally.

2 Meanwhile, cook pasta according to package directions. Drain; rinse and drain well. In a large bowl toss cooked pasta with the ³/4 cup milk, 2 of the beaten eggs, and half of the butter. Set pasta mixture aside.

3 For sauce, in a small saucepan melt remaining butter over medium heat. Stir in flour, salt, and pepper until smooth. Gradually add the 1¹/2 cups milk. Cook and stir until bubbly. Gradually stir hot mixture into 2 remaining beaten eggs. Set aside.

4 Grease a 3-quart rectangular baking dish. Spread half of the pasta mixture in the prepared dish. Top with meat sauce. Sprinkle with one-third of the cheese. Top with the remaining pasta mixture; sprinkle with another one-third of the cheese. Pour cream sauce over all; sprinkle with remaining cheese. Bake, covered, in a 350° oven for 20 minutes. Uncover; bake for 10 to 15 minutes more or until a knife inserted in center comes out clean. Let stand 15 minutes before serving (if toting, see below).

For 4 servings: Prepare as above, except assemble and bake in a 2-quart square baking dish.

To tote: Do not let stand after baking. Cover tightly. Transport in an insulated carrier.

NUTRITION FACTS PER SERVING: 431 cal., 23 g total fat (12 g sat. fat), 178 mg chol., 537 mg sodium, 30 g carbo., 2 g fiber, 23 g pro.
DAILY VALUES: 11% vit. A, 8% vit. C, 19% calcium, 13% iron

PREP: 45 minutes BAKE: 30 minutes
STAND: 15 minutes OVEN: 350°F

8 SERVINGS	INGREDIENTS	4 SERVINGS
1 lb.	lean ground beef	8 oz.
1 cup	chopped onion	¹/2 cup
1 8-oz. can	tomato sauce	¹/2 cup
¹/4 cup	dry white wine, beef broth, or water	2 Tbsp.
¹/8 tsp.	ground cinnamon	Dash
8 oz. (about 2²/3 cups)	dried penne	4 oz. (about 1¹/3 cups)
³/4 cup	milk	¹/3 cup
2	slightly beaten egg(s)	1
¹/4 cup	butter or margarine	2 Tbsp.
2 Tbsp.	all-purpose flour	1 Tbsp.
¹/4 tsp.	salt	¹/8 tsp.
¹/8 tsp.	black pepper	Dash
1¹/2 cups	milk	³/4 cup
2	slightly beaten egg(s)	1
1 cup (4 oz.)	shredded Kefalotiri, kasseri, or Romano cheese	¹/2 cup (2 oz.)

Italian Crescent Casserole

Crescent rolls pinch-hit as a crust for this casserole, cutting the time spent in the kitchen. Use your favorite brand of spaghetti or pasta sauce (including chunky vegetables, if you like) for a tailored dish.

PREP: 25 minutes
BAKE: 20 minutes OVEN: 375°F

12 SERVINGS	INGREDIENTS	6 SERVINGS
2 lb.	lean ground beef	1 lb.
1/2 cup	chopped onion	1/4 cup
2 cups	bottled spaghetti or pasta sauce	1 cup
3 cups (12 oz.)	shredded mozzarella or Monterey Jack cheese	1 1/2 cups (6 oz.)
1 8-oz. carton	dairy sour cream	1/2 cup
1 8-oz. pkg. (8)	refrigerated crescent rolls	1 4-oz. pkg. (4)
2 Tbsp.	butter or margarine, melted	1 Tbsp.
1/2 cup	grated Parmesan cheese	1/4 cup

1 In a 12-inch skillet cook ground beef and onion until meat is brown; drain off fat. Stir in spaghetti sauce; heat through. Spread meat mixture in an ungreased 3-quart rectangular baking dish.

2 Meanwhile, combine mozzarella cheese and sour cream; spoon over meat mixture in baking dish.

3 Unroll crescent rolls, but do not separate into triangles. On a lightly floured surface, press dough edges together and roll out slightly to fit dish. Place dough over the cheese layer. Brush with melted butter and sprinkle with Parmesan cheese. Bake, uncovered, in a 375° oven for 20 to 25 minutes or until top is deep golden brown.

For 6 servings: Prepare as above, except assemble and bake in an ungreased 2-quart casserole dish. (If using a round dish, separate crescent rolls into triangles and arrange on top of cheese mixture.)

To tote: Cover casserole tightly. Transport in an insulated carrier.

NUTRITION FACTS PER SERVING: 360 cal., 23 g total fat (11 g sat. fat), 81 mg chol., 593 mg sodium, 14 g carbo., 0 g fiber, 25 g pro.
DAILY VALUES: 8% vit. A, 2% vit. C, 28% calcium, 11% iron

Cheesy Pasta-Beef Bake

Sour cream, cream cheese, and cheddar cheese create a richly flavored sauce in this beefy pasta dish. The beef, pasta, and white sauce form distinct layers when served.

1 Grease two 2-quart rectangular baking dishes; set aside. Cook rotini according to package directions; drain. Meanwhile, in a large skillet cook ground beef until brown; drain off fat. Stir in tomato sauce. Bring to boiling; reduce heat. Simmer, uncovered, for 15 minutes, stirring occasionally.

2 In a small bowl combine dip, cream cheese, and milk. Layer beef mixture, cooked pasta, and dip mixture in prepared baking dishes.

3 Bake, covered, in a 350° oven for 15 minutes. Uncover and sprinkle with cheese. Bake, uncovered, for 15 minutes more. If desired, top with green onions.

For 8 servings: Prepare as above, except assemble and bake in one greased 2-quart rectangular baking dish.

To tote: Cover tightly. Transport in an insulated carrier. If desired, transport green onions in an insulated cooler with ice packs.

NUTRITION FACTS PER SERVING: 354 cal., 19 g total fat (10 g sat. fat), 71 mg chol., 613 mg sodium, 28 g carbo., 2 g fiber, 19 g pro.
DAILY VALUES: 10% vit. A, 9% vit. C, 13% calcium, 14% iron

PREP: 30 minutes
BAKE: 30 minutes OVEN: 350°F

16 SERVINGS	INGREDIENTS	8 SERVINGS
16 oz. (about 5½ cups)	dried rotini or elbow macaroni	8 oz. (about 2¾ cups)
2 lb.	lean ground beef	1 lb.
2 15-oz. cans	Italian-style tomato sauce	1 15-oz. can
2 8-oz. containers	dairy sour cream chive dip	1 8-oz. container
6 oz.	cream cheese, softened	3 oz.
¼ cup	milk	2 Tbsp.
1½ cups (6 oz.)	shredded cheddar cheese and/or mozzarella cheese	¾ cup (3 oz.)
¼ cup	sliced green onions (optional)	2 Tbsp.

Creole Lasagna

This robust Louisiana-style variation of lasagna is a tasty combination of sausage and beef with traditional lasagna ingredients. Andouille sausage, a spicy smoked variety, is perfect for this lasagna.

PREP: 35 minutes BAKE: 30 minutes
STAND: 10 minutes OVEN: 350°F

8 SERVINGS — INGREDIENTS — 6 SERVINGS

8 SERVINGS	INGREDIENTS	6 SERVINGS
8	dried lasagna noodles	6
1/2 lb.	cooked andouille sausage or smoked pork sausage links, halved lengthwise and sliced	6 oz.
1/2 lb.	lean ground beef	6 oz.
1/2 cup	chopped celery	1/3 cup
1/3 cup	chopped green sweet pepper	1/4 cup
1/3 cup	chopped onion	1/4 cup
2	clove(s) garlic, minced	1
1 1/2 cups	water	1 cup
1 6-oz. can	tomato paste	1/2 cup
2 tsp.	sugar	1 1/2 tsp.
1/4 tsp.	ground red pepper	1/8 tsp.
2 cups (8 oz.)	sliced mozzarella cheese	1 1/2 cups (6 oz.)
1/3 cup	finely shredded Parmesan cheese	1/4 cup

1 Lightly grease a 3-quart rectangular baking dish; set aside. Cook lasagna noodles according to package directions. Drain noodles; rinse with cold water. Drain well.

2 Meanwhile, for meat sauce, in a large saucepan cook sausage over medium-high heat until brown, stirring frequently. Remove sausage from pan. In the same saucepan cook ground beef, celery, sweet pepper, onion, and garlic until meat is brown and vegetables are tender. Drain off fat. Stir in sausage, water, tomato paste, sugar, and ground red pepper. Bring to boiling; reduce heat. Simmer, covered, for 15 minutes.

3 Arrange 4 of the lasagna noodles in the prepared dish. Top with half of the meat sauce and half of the cheeses. Repeat layers with remaining noodles and remaining sauce.

4 Bake, covered, in a 350° oven for 20 minutes. Uncover and top with remaining cheeses. Bake 10 minutes more. Let lasagna stand 10 minutes before serving.

For 6 servings: Prepare as above, except assemble and bake in a 2-quart rectangular baking dish. Use 3 of the lasagna noodles for each layer in step 3.

To tote: Do not let stand after baking. Cover tightly. Transport in an insulated carrier.

NUTRITION FACTS PER SERVING: 384 cal., 20 g total fat (9 g sat. fat), 63 mg chol., 615 mg sodium, 26 g carbo., 2 g fiber, 23 g pro.
DAILY VALUES: 7% vit. A, 17% vit. C, 21% calcium, 11% iron

Pizza in a Bowl

No crust required. Simply spoon this pasta mixture, which boasts all the typical pizza toppers, into a bowl to serve.

1 Cook pasta according to package directions, except omit salt; drain well. Meanwhile, cut half of the pepperoni slices into quarters; set aside.

2 In a large skillet cook ground beef and onion until meat is brown and onion is tender; drain off fat. Stir in pizza sauce, tomato sauce, tomato paste, sugar, garlic salt, and pepper. Stir in the cooked rotini and quartered pepperoni slices.

3 Spoon half of the rotini mixture into a 2-quart casserole; sprinkle with half of the mozzarella cheese. Repeat layers. Top with Parmesan cheese and remaining pepperoni slices. Bake, uncovered, in a 350° oven for 35 to 40 minutes or until heated through.

For 4 servings: Prepare as above, except assemble and bake in a 1¹/₂-quart casserole.

To tote: Cover casserole tightly. Transport in an insulated carrier.

NUTRITION FACTS PER SERVING: 521 cal., 21 g total fat (10 g sat. fat), 84 mg chol., 1,184 mg sodium, 45 g carbo., 3 g fiber, 35 g pro.
DAILY VALUES: 5% vit. A, 21% vit. C, 30% calcium, 21% iron

PREP: 30 minutes
BAKE: 35 minutes   OVEN: 350°F

6 SERVINGS	INGREDIENTS	4 SERVINGS
2 cups	dried rotini	1¹/₂ cups
1 3¹/₂-oz. pkg.	thinly sliced pepperoni	¹/₂ 3¹/₂-oz. pkg.
1 lb.	lean ground beef	12 oz.
¹/₃ cup	finely chopped onion	¹/₄ cup
1 15-oz. can	pizza sauce	1 8-oz. can
1 8-oz. can	tomato sauce	1 8-oz. can
1 6-oz. can	tomato paste	¹/₂ 6-oz. can (¹/₃ cup)
¹/₂ tsp.	sugar	¹/₄ tsp.
¹/₄ tsp.	garlic salt or onion salt	¹/₈ tsp.
¹/₈ tsp.	black pepper	Dash
2 cups (8 oz.)	shredded mozzarella cheese	1¹/₂ cups (6 oz.)
2 Tbsp.	grated Parmesan cheese	1 Tbsp.

Italian-Style Burgers

Tote these basil-scented burgers to your picnic site and grill them within 2 hours. For safety reasons, be sure to cook ground beef until no pink remains.

PREP: 15 minutes
GRILL: 14 minutes CHILL: 1 hour

INGREDIENTS

8 SERVINGS		4 SERVINGS
1/2 cup	fine dry bread crumbs	1/4 cup
1/2 cup	finely chopped onion	1/4 cup
1/3 cup	milk	3 Tbsp.
2 Tbsp.	grated Parmesan cheese	1 Tbsp.
1 Tbsp.	dried basil, crushed	1 1/2 tsp.
1/2 tsp.	garlic salt	1/4 tsp.
1/4 tsp.	black pepper	1/8 tsp.
1 1/2 lb.	lean ground beef	12 oz.
8 slices	provolone cheese	4 slices
8	kaiser rolls with sesame seeds, split and toasted	4
	Lettuce (optional)	
	Yellow or red tomato slices (optional)	
	Pasta sauce, heated (optional)	

1 In a medium bowl stir together bread crumbs, onion, milk, Parmesan cheese, basil, garlic salt, and pepper. Add meat; mix well. Shape meat mixture into eight 3/4-inch-thick patties. Place patties in a shallow container. Cover and chill for 1 hour.

2 For a charcoal grill, grill patties on the rack of an uncovered grill directly over medium coals for 14 to 18 minutes or until done (160°F), turning once halfway through grilling and topping each burger with a cheese slice during the last 1 minute. (For a gas grill, preheat grill. Reduce heat to medium. Place patties on grill rack over heat. Cover and grill as above.)

3 Serve burgers on rolls with lettuce and tomato, if desired. If desired, top with a spoonful of pasta sauce.

For 4 servings: Prepare as above, except shape meat mixture into four 3/4-inch-thick patties.

Make-ahead directions: Wrap each patty individually in freezer wrap or foil; place in an airtight container or plastic freezer bag. Seal, label, and freeze for up to 1 month. Thaw overnight in the refrigerator. Grill and serve as directed.

To tote: Transport chilled patties in an insulated cooler with ice packs. Grill within 2 hours.

NUTRITION FACTS PER SERVING: 464 cal., 22 g total fat (10 g sat. fat), 74 mg chol., 823 mg sodium, 36 g carbo., 2 g fiber, 29 g pro.
DAILY VALUES: 6% vit. A, 1% vit. C, 32% calcium, 21% iron

Pioneer Beans and Beef

If you like barbecued beans, you'll love this dish. Three types of beans, beef, bacon, molasses, and brown sugar combine for a tasty dish.

PREP: 20 minutes
BAKE: 1 hour   OVEN: 350°F

8 SERVINGS — INGREDIENTS — 4 SERVINGS

8 Servings	Ingredients	4 Servings
1 lb.	ground beef	8 oz.
4 slices	bacon, chopped	2 slices
½ cup	chopped onion	¼ cup
1 15-oz. can	red kidney beans, rinsed and drained	½ 15-oz. can
1 15-oz. can	butter beans, rinsed and drained	1 8-oz. can
1 15-oz. can	pork and beans in tomato sauce, undrained	1 8-oz. can
1 cup	catsup	½ cup
⅓ cup	packed brown sugar	3 Tbsp.
¼ cup	mild-flavored molasses	2 Tbsp.
1 Tbsp.	vinegar	1½ tsp.
1 Tbsp.	prepared mustard	1½ tsp.

1 In a large skillet cook the ground beef, bacon, and onion until meat is brown and onion is tender; drain off fat. Stir in kidney beans, butter beans, pork and beans, catsup, brown sugar, molasses, vinegar, and mustard.

2 Transfer to a 2- to 2½-quart casserole. Bake, covered, in a 350° oven for 30 minutes. Uncover and bake for 30 minutes more.

Slow cooker directions: For the 8-serving recipe, prepare as directed, except transfer meat and bean mixture to a 3½- or 4-quart slow cooker. Cover and cook on low-heat setting for 5 to 6 hours or on high-heat setting for 2½ to 3 hours. (Do not use slow cooker for 4-serving recipe.)

For 4 servings: Prepare as above, except transfer bean mixture to a 1-quart casserole. Bake, covered, in a 350° oven for 30 minutes. Uncover and bake for 15 to 20 minutes more.

To tote: Cover tightly. Transport in an insulated carrier. (Or, if desired, transport slow cooker in an insulated carrier.)

NUTRITION FACTS PER SERVING: 357 cal., 9 g total fat (4 g sat. fat), 42 mg chol., 982 mg sodium, 51 g carbo., 8 g fiber, 22 g pro.
DAILY VALUES: 7% vit. A, 11% vit. C, 10% calcium, 28% iron

Shepherd's Pie

This classic dish is a welcome addition to a potluck gathering. For the mashed potatoes, use leftover or purchased refrigerated or frozen mashed potatoes.

PREP: 30 minutes BAKE: 40 minutes
STAND: 10 minutes OVEN: 400°F

INGREDIENTS

8 SERVINGS		6 SERVINGS
¹/₄ cup	butter or margarine	3 Tbsp.
¹/₄ cup	all-purpose flour	3 Tbsp.
1 tsp.	dried thyme, crushed	³/₄ tsp.
¹/₄ tsp.	black pepper	¹/₈ tsp.
1 cup	beef broth	²/₃ cup
²/₃ cup	milk	¹/₂ cup
4 cups (20 oz.)	cubed cooked lamb or beef	3 cups (1 lb.)
1 16-oz. pkg.	frozen mixed vegetables, thawed and drained	1 10-oz. pkg.
1¹/₂ cups	frozen small whole onions, thawed and drained	1 cup
3¹/₂ cups	prepared mashed potatoes	2²/₃ cups
³/₄ cup (3 oz.)	shredded cheddar cheese	¹/₂ cup (2 oz.)

1 In a 4-quart Dutch oven melt butter; stir in flour, thyme, and pepper. Stir in broth and milk all at once. Cook and stir over medium heat until thickened and bubbly. Remove from heat. Stir in meat, vegetables, and onions. Transfer to a 3-quart casserole. Spoon mashed potatoes around the edge.

2 Bake, uncovered, in a 400° oven for 35 minutes. Remove from oven and sprinkle with cheddar cheese. Bake, uncovered, about 5 minutes more or until bubbly and potatoes are brown. Let stand for 10 minutes before serving (if toting, see below).

For 6 servings: Prepare as above, except use a large saucepan for meat mixture. Assemble and bake in a 2-quart casserole.

To tote: Do not let stand after baking. Cover tightly. Transport in an insulated carrier.

NUTRITION FACTS PER SERVING: 377 cal., 16 g total fat (9 g sat. fat), 94 mg chol., 578 mg sodium, 31 g carbo., 5 g fiber, 28 g pro.
DAILY VALUES: 64% vit. A, 21% vit. C, 18% calcium, 15% iron

Tacos in Pasta Shells

Just six ingredients make up these shells. But better than that, they appeal to the entire family.

PREP: 40 minutes
BAKE: 30 minutes OVEN: 350°F

12 SERVINGS	INGREDIENTS	6 SERVINGS
1 12-oz. pkg. (about 36)	dried jumbo shell macaroni	1/2 12-oz. pkg. (about 18)
2 1/2 lb.	ground beef	1 1/4 lb.
6 oz.	cream cheese, cut up	1 3-oz. pkg.
2 tsp.	chili powder	1 tsp.
2 16-oz. jars	salsa	1 16-oz. jar
1 1/2 cups (6 oz.)	shredded cheddar cheese	3/4 cup (3 oz.)
	Chopped tomato (optional)	
	Sliced pitted ripe olives (optional)	

1 Cook shells according to package directions. Drain shells; rinse with cold water. Drain well.

2 Meanwhile, in a large skillet cook ground beef until brown; drain off fat. Stir in cream cheese and chili powder. Remove from heat; cool slightly. Divide beef mixture evenly among the cooked shells.

3 Spread about 1/2 cup salsa into each of two 2-quart rectangular baking dishes. Arrange filled shells in dishes; top with remaining salsa.

4 Bake, covered, in a 350° oven for 15 minutes. Remove from oven and sprinkle with cheddar cheese. Bake, uncovered, about 15 minutes more or until heated through. If desired, sprinkle with tomato and olives.

For 6 servings: Prepare using the method above, except assemble and bake in one 2-quart rectangular baking dish.

To tote: Cover tightly. Transport in an insulated carrier. If desired, transport tomato and olives in an insulated cooler with ice packs.

NUTRITION FACTS PER SERVING: 416 cal., 22 g total fat (11 g sat. fat), 90 mg chol., 513 mg sodium, 27 g carbo., 2 g fiber, 27 g pro.
DAILY VALUES: 19% vit. A, 18% vit. C, 15% calcium, 20% iron

Italian Beef Sandwiches

The meat for these sandwiches is cooked in a slow cooker. Let it cook all day for an evening gathering. For a crowd, use small dinner rolls to make the meat go farther.

1 Place beef in a 3^1/$_2$-, 4-, or 5-quart slow cooker. Stir together water, salad dressing mix, Italian seasoning, crushed red pepper, and garlic powder; pour over beef in slow cooker. Cover and cook on low-heat setting for 10 to 12 hours or on high-heat setting for 5 to 6 hours.

2 Remove meat with a slotted spoon. Using two forks, shred the meat. Serve meat on rolls. Drizzle each sandwich with some of the juices to moisten. If desired, top each sandwich with roasted red pepper strips.

For 8 sandwiches: Prepare using the method above, except assemble and cook in a 3^1/$_2$- or 4-quart slow cooker.

To tote: Return shredded meat to slow cooker. Transport slow cooker in an insulated carrier. (Or, if desired, transfer shredded meat and juices to a serving dish. Cover tightly. Transport in an insulated carrier.) If desired, transport roasted red pepper strips in an airtight container. Serve meat with a slotted spoon.

NUTRITION FACTS PER SERVING: 361 cal., 8 g total fat (2 g sat. fat), 91 mg chol., 598 mg sodium, 31 g carbo., 1 g fiber, 38 g pro.
DAILY VALUES: 7% calcium, 34% iron

PREP: 10 minutes COOK: 5 or 10 hours

12 SERVINGS	INGREDIENTS	8 SERVINGS
1 4-lb.	boneless beef sirloin or rump roast, cut into 2- to 3-inch pieces	1 3-lb.
^{1}/$_2$ cup	water	^{1}/$_3$ cup
1 0.7-oz. pkg.	Italian dry salad dressing mix	1 0.7-oz. pkg.
2 tsp.	Italian seasoning, crushed	1 tsp.
^{1}/$_2$ to 1 tsp.	crushed red pepper	^{1}/$_4$ to ^{1}/$_2$ tsp.
^{1}/$_2$ tsp.	garlic powder	^{1}/$_4$ tsp.
12	kaiser rolls or other sandwich rolls, split	8
	Roasted red sweet pepper strips (optional)	

Bean and Beef Enchilada Casserole

Consider this hearty casserole as comfort food with a south-of-the-border twist. It is the perfect dish to come home to after a long day.

1 In a large skillet cook the ground beef and onion until meat is brown and onion is tender; drain off fat. Stir in chili powder and cumin; cook and stir 1 minute more. Stir pinto beans and undrained chile peppers into meat mixture; set aside. In a small bowl stir together sour cream, flour, and garlic powder; set aside.

2 Place half of the tortillas in the bottom of a lightly greased 3-quart rectangular baking dish, cutting to fit and overlapping as necessary. Top with half of the meat mixture, half of the sour cream mixture, and half of the enchilada sauce. Repeat layers.

3 Bake, covered, in a 350° oven for 35 to 40 minutes or until heated through. Uncover and sprinkle with cheese. Bake about 5 minutes more or until cheese is melted. If desired, garnish with cilantro and fresh chile peppers.

For 8 servings: Prepare as above, except assemble and bake in a 2-quart rectangular baking dish.

To tote: Cover tightly. Transport in an insulated carrier. If desired, transport cilantro and chile peppers in an airtight container.

NUTRITION FACTS PER SERVING: 304 cal., 14 g total fat (7 g sat. fat), 38 mg chol., 682 mg sodium, 32 g carbo., 6 g fiber, 15 g pro.
DAILY VALUES: 11% vit. A, 14% vit. C, 18% calcium, 17% iron

PREP: 35 minutes
BAKE: 40 minutes OVEN: 350°F

INGREDIENTS

12 SERVINGS		8 SERVINGS
12 oz.	lean ground beef	8 oz.
3/4 cup	chopped onion	1/2 cup
1 1/2 tsp.	chili powder	1 tsp.
3/4 tsp.	ground cumin	1/2 tsp.
2 15-oz. cans	pinto beans, rinsed and drained	1 15-oz. can
2 4-oz. cans	diced green chile peppers, undrained	1 4-oz. can
1 1/2 cups	dairy sour cream	1 8-oz. carton
3 Tbsp.	all-purpose flour	2 Tbsp.
1/2 tsp.	garlic powder	1/4 tsp.
12 6-inch	corn tortillas	8 6-inch
2 10-oz. cans	enchilada sauce	1 10-oz. can
1 cup (4 oz.)	shredded cheddar cheese	3/4 cup (3 oz.)
	Fresh cilantro and Red chile peppers, sliced (optional)	

Down-South Barbecue Sandwiches

This recipe features both beef and pork—which are cooked to tender perfection and shredded—and feeds a crowd of hungry tailgaters.

PREP: 15 minutes   COOK: 2½ hours

16 SERVINGS	INGREDIENTS	8 SERVINGS
1 cup	water	½ cup
1 6-oz. can	tomato paste	½ 6-oz. can (⅓ cup)
½ cup	packed brown sugar	¼ cup
¼ cup	cider vinegar	2 Tbsp.
2 Tbsp.	chili powder	1 Tbsp.
2 tsp.	Worcestershire sauce	1 tsp.
1 tsp.	dry mustard	½ tsp.
1½ lb.	boneless beef chuck roast	¾ lb.
1½ lb.	boneless pork shoulder roast	¾ lb.
16	hamburger buns, split and toasted	8

1 For sauce, in a 4-quart Dutch oven combine water, tomato paste, brown sugar, vinegar, chili powder, Worcestershire sauce, and dry mustard. Add beef and pork roasts to sauce, cutting meat to fit in Dutch oven, if necessary.

2 Bring to boiling; reduce heat. Simmer, covered, about 2½ hours or until meat is very tender, stirring occasionally.

3 Remove meat from pan, reserving sauce in Dutch oven. Shred meat with two forks. Stir shredded meat into sauce in Dutch oven. Serve meat mixture on buns.

Slow cooker directions: For the 16-sandwich recipe, use ingredient amounts listed, except reduce water in sauce to ¼ cup. Place beef and pork roasts in a 3½- or 4-quart slow cooker, cutting meat to fit, if necessary. Pour sauce over meat in cooker. Cover and cook on low-heat setting for 10 to 12 hours or on high-heat setting for 5 to 6 hours. Remove meat from slow cooker, reserving sauce. Shred meat with two forks. Stir together shredded meat and reserved sauce in cooker. (Do not use slow cooker for 8-sandwich recipe.)

For 8 sandwiches: Prepare as above, except cook meat in a 3-quart saucepan and simmer, covered, for 1½ to 2 hours or until very tender, stirring occasionally.

To tote: Transfer meat mixture to serving dish. Cover tightly. Transport in an insulated carrier. (Or, if desired, transport slow cooker in an insulated carrier.)

NUTRITION FACTS PER SERVING: 286 cal., 8 g total fat (3 g sat. fat), 56 mg chol., 330 mg sodium, 31 g carbo., 2 g fiber, 21 g pro.
DAILY VALUES: 7% vit. A, 5% vit. C, 8% calcium, 19% iron

Cheesy Sausage and Rice Bake

Crisp rice cereal is a surprising ingredient in this tasty casserole.

1 Grease a 3-quart rectangular baking dish; set dish aside.

2 Cook sausage and onion in a 12-inch skillet until sausage is brown and onion is tender; drain off fat. Set sausage mixture aside.

3 Meanwhile, in a large bowl combine 5 cups of the cereal and the cooked rice. Spread rice mixture evenly in the bottom of the prepared baking dish. Spoon sausage mixture over rice layer. Sprinkle with cheddar cheese.

4 In a medium mixing bowl beat eggs, soup, and milk with a wire whisk until combined; carefully pour over layers in baking dish. Press down lightly with the back of a spoon. Toss the remaining 1 cup cereal with the melted butter; sprinkle over the top.

5 Bake, uncovered, in a 325° oven for 45 to 50 minutes or until bubbly and golden brown. Let stand 10 minutes before serving.

For 6 servings: Prepare as above, except assemble and bake in a greased 2-quart square baking dish.

To tote: Do not let casserole stand after baking. Cover tightly. Transport in an insulated carrier.

NUTRITION FACTS PER SERVING: 490 cal., 33 g total fat (14 g sat. fat), 175 mg chol., 872 mg sodium, 24 g carbo., 0 g fiber, 19 g pro.
DAILY VALUES: 14% vit. A, 12% vit. C, 18% calcium, 11% iron

PREP: 25 minutes BAKE: 45 minutes
STAND: 10 minutes OVEN: 325°F

12 SERVINGS	INGREDIENTS	**6** SERVINGS
2 lb.	mild and/or hot bulk pork sausage	1 lb.
½ cup	chopped onion	¼ cup
6 cups	crisp rice cereal	3 cups
1½ cups	cooked white rice	¾ cup
2 cups (8 oz.)	shredded cheddar cheese	1 cup (4 oz.)
6	eggs	3
2 10¾-oz. cans	reduced-sodium condensed cream of celery soup	1 10¾-oz. can
½ cup	milk	¼ cup
1 Tbsp.	butter or margarine, melted	1½ tsp.

Southwest Spaghetti Pie

This pie will be a hit at any potluck with kids present! Cooked spaghetti makes up the crust. The topping is loaded with cheese, tomato sauce, and ground pork.

PREP: 40 minutes   BAKE: 10 minutes
STAND: 5 minutes   OVEN: 425°F

8 SERVINGS	INGREDIENTS	4 SERVINGS
8 oz.	dried spaghetti	4 oz.
1/2 cup	milk	1/4 cup
1	egg	1
1 lb.	ground pork	8 oz.
1 cup	chopped onion	1/2 cup
3/4 cup	chopped green sweet pepper	1/3 cup
1 clove	garlic, minced	1 small clove
1 Tbsp.	chili powder	1 1/2 tsp.
1/2 tsp.	salt	1/4 tsp.
1/2 tsp.	ground cumin	1/4 tsp.
1/2 tsp.	dried oregano, crushed	1/4 tsp.
1/4 tsp.	black pepper	1/8 tsp.
1 15-oz. can	tomato sauce	1 8-oz. can
1 cup (4 oz.)	shredded Monterey Jack cheese with jalapeño peppers	1/2 cup (2 oz.)
1 cup (4 oz.)	shredded cheddar cheese	1/2 cup (2 oz.)

1 Cook spaghetti according to package directions; drain well. Return to pan. Combine milk and egg; stir into hot pasta. Transfer to a buttered 3-quart rectangular baking dish (there will be some liquid).

2 Meanwhile, in a large skillet cook pork, onion, sweet pepper, and garlic until meat is brown; drain off fat. Stir in chili powder, salt, cumin, oregano, and pepper. Cook and stir for 2 minutes. Stir in tomato sauce. Bring to boiling; reduce heat. Simmer, uncovered, for 2 minutes more. Spoon over pasta in baking dish. Sprinkle with cheeses.

3 Bake, uncovered, in a 425° oven about 10 minutes or until bubbly around the edges. Let stand 5 minutes before serving (if toting, see below).

For 4 servings: Prepare as above, except assemble and bake in a 9-inch pie plate.

To tote: Do not let stand after baking. Cover tightly. Transport in an insulated carrier.

NUTRITION FACTS PER SERVING: 330 cal., 15 g total fat (8 g sat. fat), 84 mg chol., 621 mg sodium, 29 g carbo., 2 g fiber, 20 g pro.
DAILY VALUES: 17% vit. A, 20% vit. C, 24% calcium, 11% iron

Creamy Cabbage and Sausage

Cabbage lovers will enjoy this recipe. Sour cream and American cheese create a creamy dish, and the pork sausage adds flavor and spice.

1 In a Dutch oven cook sausage and onion over medium-high heat until sausage is brown. Drain off fat. Stir in cabbage. Cook, covered, over medium heat about 10 minutes or until cabbage is crisp-tender, stirring occasionally. Drain off any excess liquid.

2 Stir in sour cream, cheese, salt, and pepper. Transfer sausage mixture to a 3-quart rectangular baking dish.

3 In a small bowl, combine bread crumbs and melted butter or margarine; sprinkle over sausage mixture. Bake, uncovered, in a 375° oven for 20 minutes or until bread crumbs are golden.

For 4 servings: Prepare as above, except use a very large ovenproof skillet; add bread crumb topping and bake in skillet 20 minutes.

To tote: Cover hot mixture tightly; tote in an insulated carrier.

NUTRITION FACTS PER SERVING: 520 cal., 42 g total fat (21 g sat. fat), 93 mg chol., 902 mg sodium, 12 g carbo., 2 g fiber, 18 g pro.
DAILY VALUES: 15% vit. A, 43% vit. C, 24% calcium, 8% iron

PREP: 35 minutes
BAKE: 20 minutes   OVEN: 375°F

8 SERVINGS — INGREDIENTS — 4 SERVINGS

8 SERVINGS	INGREDIENTS	4 SERVINGS
1¹/₂ lb.	bulk pork sausage	³/₄ lb.
³/₄ cup	chopped onion	¹/₃ cup
10 cups	coarsely chopped cabbage	5 cups
1¹/₂ cups	dairy sour cream	³/₄ cup
1¹/₂ cups (6 oz.)	shredded American cheese	³/₄ cup (3 oz.)
¹/₄ tsp.	salt	¹/₈ tsp.
¹/₄ tsp.	black pepper	¹/₈ tsp.
1¹/₂ cups	soft bread crumbs	³/₄ cup
2 Tbsp.	butter or margarine, melted	1 Tbsp.

Zucchini-Sausage Casserole

A stuffing mixture creates a bottom layer and topper for this tasty dish. It's a great way to use your summer crop of zucchini.

PREP: 25 minutes
BAKE: 30 minutes   OVEN: 350°F

INGREDIENTS

8 SERVINGS		4 SERVINGS
1 lb.	bulk pork sausage	8 oz.
4 medium	zucchini	2 medium
1 10³/₄-oz. can	condensed cream of chicken soup	½ 10³/₄-oz. can (²/₃ cup)
1 8-oz. carton	dairy sour cream	½ cup
4 cups	chicken flavor stuffing mix	2 cups
¹/₃ cup	butter or margarine, melted	3 Tbsp.
	Nonstick cooking spray	

1 In a 12-inch skillet cook sausage until brown; drain off fat. Return sausage to skillet.

2 Meanwhile, quarter zucchini lengthwise; cut each quarter crosswise into ¹/₂-inch slices. Add zucchini to skillet.

3 In a small bowl combine soup and sour cream; stir into sausage-zucchini mixture. Set aside. In a large bowl combine stuffing mix and melted butter.

4 Lightly coat a 3-quart rectangular baking dish with cooking spray. Spoon half of the stuffing mixture into the prepared dish. Spread sausage-zucchini mixture over stuffing. Spoon remaining stuffing evenly over the top. Bake, covered, in a 350° oven about 30 minutes or until heated through.

For 4 servings: Prepare as above, except assemble and bake in a 2-quart square baking dish.

To tote: Cover casserole tightly. Transport in an insulated carrier.

NUTRITION FACTS PER SERVING: 487 cal., 34 g total fat (16 g sat. fat), 70 mg chol., 1,128 mg sodium, 28 g carbo., 2 g fiber, 14 g pro.
DAILY VALUES: 20% vit. A, 14% vit. C, 9% calcium, 11% iron

Sausage-Rice Casserole

Tailor this recipe to your heat tolerance. If spicy food is your style, use more hot Italian sausage and less sweet. Or use all of one or the other.

PREP: 25 minutes
BAKE: 50 minutes OVEN: 350°F

INGREDIENTS

12 SERVINGS		6 SERVINGS
2 lb.	uncooked sweet (mild) and/or hot Italian sausage links (remove casings, if present)	1 lb.
1 cup	chopped onion	½ cup
5 cups	cooked white rice	2½ cups
2 4-oz. cans	chopped green chile peppers, drained	1 4-oz. can
2 4-oz. cans	mushroom stems and pieces, drained	1 4-oz. can
2 10¾-oz. cans	condensed cream of chicken soup	1 10¾-oz. can
2 cups	milk	1 cup
1½ cups (6 oz.)	shredded cheddar cheese	¾ cup (3 oz.)

1 Cook sausage and onion in a 12-inch skillet until sausage is brown, stirring to break up sausage; drain off fat.

2 Meanwhile, in an extra-large bowl stir together rice, chile peppers, and mushrooms. Stir in soup, milk, and cheddar cheese. Stir in cooked sausage mixture. Divide mixture evenly between two 2-quart baking dishes. Bake, covered, in a 350° oven about 50 minutes or until heated through.

For 6 servings: Prepare using method above, except spoon mixture into one 2-quart rectangular baking dish.

Make-ahead directions: Prepare as directed. Cover and chill for up to 24 hours. Bake, covered, in a 350° oven for 65 to 70 minutes or until heated through.

To tote: Transport in an insulated carrier.

NUTRITION FACTS PER SERVING: 442 cal., 26 g total fat (11 g sat. fat), 73 mg chol., 1,056 mg sodium, 28 g carbo., 1 g fiber, 20 g pro.
DAILY VALUES: 9% vit. A, 13% vit. C, 21% calcium, 11% iron

German-Style Sausage and Potatoes

Sausage and cabbage transform a favorite side dish into a hearty main dish. Mustard and a crushed combination of aromatic seeds punches up the flavor.

1 In a Dutch oven cook potatoes, covered, in a small amount of boiling water for 20 to 25 minutes or until tender; drain. Cool, peel, and thinly slice. Using a mortar and pestle, coarsely crush the spice seeds. Combine seeds, beer, vinegar, mustard, cornstarch, and sugar; set aside.

2 In a large skillet cook onion, celery, and cabbage in hot oil for 5 to 8 minutes or just until crisp-tender.

3 In two ungreased 2-quart rectangular or square baking dishes, layer one-fourth of the cabbage mixture, one-fourth of the sausage, one-fourth of the potatoes, and one-fourth of the cheese. Stir seed mixture; divide the mixture among both dishes, spreading over the cheese. Repeat layers, reserving the cheese. Bake, uncovered, in a 375° oven for 30 to 35 minutes or until heated through. Top with reserved cheese.

For 6 servings: Prepare as above except use a large saucepan to cook potatoes. Layer half of the cabbage mixture, sausage, potatoes, cheese, and all of the seed mixture in one 2-quart rectangular or square baking dish. Repeat layers, reserving the cheese. Bake as above. Top with reserved cheese.

To tote: Cover and transport in an insulated carrier.

NUTRITION FACTS PER SERVING: 415 cal., 25 g total fat (10 g sat. fat), 57 mg chol., 670 mg sodium, 31 g carbo., 3 g fiber, 17 g pro.
DAILY VALUES: 38% vit. C, 24% calcium, 17% iron

PREP: 35 minutes COOK: 20 minutes

12 SERVINGS	INGREDIENTS	6 SERVINGS
3 lb.	medium potatoes	1½ lb.
2 Tbsp.	anise seed	1 Tbsp.
3 tsp.	caraway seed	1 tsp.
2 tsp.	mustard seed	1 tsp.
²/₃ cup	beer	¹/₃ cup
½ cup	vinegar	¼ cup
⅓ cup	spicy brown mustard	3 Tbsp.
2 Tbsp.	cornstarch	1 Tbsp.
2 Tbsp.	sugar	1 Tbsp.
2 cups	chopped onions	1 cup
2 cups	sliced celery	1 cup
2 cups	shredded cabbage	1 cup
2 Tbsp.	olive oil	1 Tbsp.
1½ lb.	fully cooked Pollish sausage, cut into ½-inch-thick slices	12 oz.
2 cups	shredded Swiss cheese	1 cup

Italian Penne Bake

This homey casserole contains all the great pasta dish ingredients—marinara sauce, mushrooms, onion, green sweet pepper, pepperoni, and lots of cheese.

1 Lightly coat a 3-quart rectangular baking dish with cooking spray; set dish aside. Cook pasta according to package directions; drain well. Return pasta to saucepan. Meanwhile, in a large skillet cook mushrooms, onion, sweet peppers, pepperoni, and garlic in hot oil for 3 minutes. Add vegetable mixture and marinara sauce to pasta; toss to coat. Spread pasta mixture evenly in prepared baking dish.

2 Bake, covered, in a 350° oven about 25 minutes or until heated through. Uncover and sprinkle with cheese. Bake, uncovered, about 5 minutes more or until cheese is melted.

For 4 servings: Prepare using method above, except assemble and bake in a 2-quart square baking dish.

To tote: Cover casserole tightly. Transport in an insulated carrier.

NUTRITION FACTS PER SERVING: 373 cal., 17 g total fat (6 g sat. fat), 27 mg chol., 905 mg sodium, 40 g carbo., 3 g fiber, 16 g pro.
DAILY VALUES: 13% vit. A, 53% vit. C, 15% calcium, 13% iron

PREP: 25 minutes
BAKE: 30 minutes   OVEN: 350°F

8 SERVINGS — INGREDIENTS — 4 SERVINGS

8 SERVINGS	INGREDIENTS	4 SERVINGS
	Nonstick cooking spray	
3 cups	dried penne	1 1/2 cups
1 cup	sliced fresh mushrooms	1/2 cup
1 cup	quartered, thinly sliced onion	1/2 cup
2 medium	green or red sweet pepper(s), cut into thin, bite-size strips	1 medium
6 oz.	sliced pepperoni or Canadian-style bacon, cut up	3 oz.
1 Tbsp.	bottled minced garlic	1 1/2 tsp.
1 Tbsp.	olive oil or cooking oil	1 1/2 tsp.
1 26- to 29-oz. jar (3 cups)	marinara pasta sauce	1 1/2 cups
1 1/4 cups (5 oz.)	shredded Italian blend cheese	2/3 cup (3 oz.)

Chili Dogs

This spicy tomato mixture for hot dogs was created in 1933 by The Coney Island Lunch Room in Grand Island, Nebraska. The recipe remains a favorite among customers.

PREP: 20 minutes   COOK: 35 minutes

8 SERVINGS — INGREDIENTS — 4 SERVINGS

8 SERVINGS	INGREDIENTS	4 SERVINGS
1 14¹/₂-oz. can	tomatoes, undrained	1 14¹/₂-oz. can
1 medium	green sweet pepper, cut up	1 medium
1 4-oz. can	diced green chile peppers, drained	1 4-oz. can
1 medium	onion, quartered	1 medium
2 tsp.	chili powder	2 tsp.
2 tsp.	paprika	2 tsp.
¹/₂ tsp.	salt	¹/₂ tsp.
¹/₂ tsp.	ground cumin	¹/₂ tsp.
¹/₂ tsp.	garlic powder	¹/₂ tsp.
¹/₄ tsp.	ground red pepper	¹/₄ tsp.
8	frankfurters	4
8	frankfurter buns	4
	Chopped onion	
	Prepared mustard	

1 For sauce, in a food processor bowl or blender container combine the tomatoes, sweet pepper, drained chile peppers, the quartered onion, chili powder, paprika, salt, cumin, garlic powder, and ground red pepper. Cover and blend or process until nearly smooth. Transfer to a large saucepan. Bring sauce to boiling; reduce heat. Simmer, covered, for 30 minutes.

2 To serve, combine 1 cup of the sauce and the 8 frankfurters in a medium saucepan. Heat through. Serve franks and sauce on buns with onion and mustard. Store remaining sauce in refrigerator or freezer (see make-ahead directions).

For 4 chili dogs: Prepare as above, except add ¹/₂ cup of the sauce to the 4 frankfurters.

Make-ahead directions: Prepare sauce; cool. Store in an airtight container in the refrigerator for up to 3 days or in freezer for 3 months.

To tote: Transfer frankfurters and sauce to a serving container or 3¹/₂-quart slow cooker. Cover tightly. Transport in an insulated carrier. Serve within 1 hour.

NUTRITION FACTS PER SERVING: 320 cal., 18 g total fat (7 g sat. fat), 29 mg chol., 1,057 mg sodium, 27 g carbo., 2 g fiber, 10 g pro.
DAILY VALUES: 10% vit. A, 21% vit. C, 5% calcium, 12% iron

Mexican Rice and Black Bean Casserole

Pork sausage and spices from the Mexican-style stewed tomatoes give this casserole its punch of flavor. For more heat, use shredded Monterey Jack cheese with jalapeños instead of cheddar.

1 In a 12-inch skillet cook sausage until brown; drain off fat. Stir in tomatoes, cooked rice, black beans, and sweet pepper. Spoon into a 3-quart rectangular baking dish.

2 Bake, covered, in a 350° oven for 40 to 45 minutes or until heated through. Remove from oven and sprinkle with cheese. Let stand 5 minutes before serving (if toting, see below). If desired, serve with sour cream.

For 4 servings: Prepare as above, except cook sausage in a 10-inch skillet, spoon into a 2-quart square baking dish, and bake for 30 to 35 minutes.

To tote: Do not let stand after baking. Cover casserole tightly. Transport in an insulated carrier. If desired, transport sour cream in an insulated cooler with ice packs.

NUTRITION FACTS PER SERVING: 343 cal., 19 g total fat (8 g sat. fat), 40 mg chol., 811 mg sodium, 27 g carbo., 3 g fiber, 14 g pro.
DAILY VALUES: 3% vit. A, 45% vit. C, 10% calcium, 10% iron

PREP: 20 minutes BAKE: 40 minutes
STAND: 5 minutes OVEN: 350°F

8 SERVINGS	INGREDIENTS	4 SERVINGS
1 lb.	bulk pork sausage	8 oz.
2 14½-oz. cans	Mexican-style stewed tomatoes, undrained	1 14½-oz. can
2 cups	cooked white rice	1 cup
1 15-oz. can	black beans, rinsed and drained	1 15-oz. can
1 medium	green sweet pepper, coarsely chopped	½ medium
½ cup (2 oz.)	shredded cheddar cheese	¼ cup (1 oz.)
	Dairy sour cream (optional)	

Best-Ever Chili with Beans

This chili travels well in a slow cooker or deep casserole dish. Italian sausage and beef cubes provide heartiness. Bacon adds an interesting flavor note.

PREP: 45 minutes COOK: 1¼ hours

12 SERVINGS	INGREDIENTS	6 SERVINGS
1 lb.	uncooked Italian sausage links (remove casings, if present)	½ lb.
3 lb.	boneless beef chuck roast, cut into ½-inch cubes	1½ lb.
1½ cups	chopped green sweet pepper	¾ cup
5 cups	water	2½ cups
2 15-oz. cans	pinto or kidney beans, rinsed and drained	1 15-oz. can
2 14½-oz. cans	diced tomatoes with onion and garlic, undrained	1 14½-oz. can
2 6-oz. cans	tomato paste or Italian-style tomato paste	1 6-oz. can
2 Tbsp.	chili powder	1 Tbsp.
2 to 3	fresh jalapeño chile pepper(s), seeded and finely chopped	1 to 2
½ tsp.	salt	¼ tsp.
12 slices	bacon, crisp-cooked, drained, and crumbled	6 slices

1 In a 6-quart Dutch oven cook sausage until brown. Remove with a slotted spoon, reserving drippings in Dutch oven. Cook half of the beef cubes in the hot drippings until meat is brown; remove meat from pan. Add remaining beef cubes and sweet pepper. Cook until meat is brown; drain off fat. Return all meat to Dutch oven.

2 Stir in the water, beans, tomatoes, tomato paste, chili powder, jalapeño peppers, and salt. Bring to boiling; reduce heat. Simmer, covered, about 1¼ hours or until meat is tender. Stir in bacon; heat through.

Slow cooker directions: For the 12-serving recipe, brown sausage and beef cubes as directed. Combine all ingredients except bacon in a 3½-, 4- or 5-quart slow cooker. Cover and cook on low-heat setting for 8 to 10 hours or on high-heat setting for 4 to 5 hours. Stir in bacon before serving; heat through. (Do not use slow cooker for 6-serving recipe.)

To tote: Transfer to a serving dish. Cover tightly. Transport in an insulated carrier. (Or, if desired, transport slow cooker in an insulated carrier.)

NUTRITION FACTS PER SERVING: 510 cal., 30 g total fat (11 g sat. fat), 104 mg chol., 1,064 mg sodium, 24 g carbo., 6 g fiber, 36 g pro.
DAILY VALUES: 11% vit. A, 45% vit. C, 5% calcium, 28% iron

Spinach and Ham Lasagna

Deviate from the traditional red-sauced lasagna. This luscious lasagna is layered with spinach, ham, cheese, and a lightened "cream" sauce. Ham adds a tasty smoky flavor.

1 Cook lasagna noodles according to package directions. Drain noodles; rinse with cold water. Drain well.

2 Meanwhile, for sauce, in a medium saucepan combine the milk, onion, cornstarch, and salt. Cook and stir until thickened and bubbly. Cook and stir 2 minutes more. Spread 2 tablespoons of the sauce evenly on the bottom of a 3-quart rectangular baking dish. Stir ham and Italian seasoning into remaining sauce.

3 Arrange half of the lasagna noodles in the dish. Spread with one-third of the remaining sauce. Top with the spinach. Layer another one-third of the sauce, the cottage cheese, and half of the mozzarella cheese over the spinach. Place remaining noodles on top. Top with remaining sauce and remaining mozzarella cheese.

4 Bake, uncovered, in a 375° oven for 30 to 35 minutes or until heated through. Let stand 10 minutes before serving (if toting, see below).

For 6 servings: Prepare using method above, except assemble and bake in a 2-quart rectangular baking dish.

To tote: Do not let stand after baking. Cover tightly. Transport in an insulated carrier.

NUTRITION FACTS PER SERVING: 237 cal., 7 g total fat (4 g sat. fat), 34 mg chol., 772 mg sodium, 23 g carbo., 2 g fiber, 20 g pro.
DAILY VALUES: 90% vit. A, 31% vit. C, 28% calcium, 12% iron

PREP: 40 minutes   BAKE: 30 minutes
STAND: 10 minutes   OVEN: 375°F

10 SERVINGS	INGREDIENTS	6 SERVINGS
8	dried lasagna noodles	6
3 cups	milk	2 cups
1/3 cup	chopped onion	1/4 cup
1/4 cup	cornstarch	3 Tbsp.
1/2 tsp.	salt	1/4 tsp.
2 1/4 cups (12 oz.)	diced low-fat, reduced-sodium cooked ham	1 1/2 cups (8 oz.)
1 tsp.	dried Italian seasoning, crushed	1/2 tsp.
2 10-oz. pkgs.	frozen chopped spinach, thawed and well drained	1 10-oz. pkg.
1 1/2 cups	cottage cheese	1 cup
1 1/2 cups (6 oz.)	shredded mozzarella cheese	1 cup (4 oz.)

Ham and Cheese Macaroni

Macaroni and cheese with a twist—ham and broccoli. A little red sweet pepper also adds flavor interest.

PREP: 30 minutes
BAKE: 45 minutes OVEN: 350°F

1 Cook macaroni according to package directions, adding broccoli and sweet pepper for the last 2 minutes of cooking; drain. In a 3-quart casserole combine macaroni mixture and ham; set aside.

2 For sauce, in a small saucepan stir together milk, cornstarch, and pepper. Cook and stir until thickened and bubbly. Add cheese; stir until melted. Stir sauce into macaroni mixture in casserole. Combine bread crumbs and butter; sprinkle over casserole.

3 Bake, uncovered, in a 350° oven about 45 minutes or until bubbly and bread crumbs are lightly browned.

For 4 servings: Prepare as above, except assemble and bake in a 2-quart casserole. Bake, uncovered, about 30 minutes or until bubbly and bread crumbs are lightly browned.

To tote: Cover casserole tightly. Transport in an insulated carrier.

NUTRITION FACTS PER SERVING: 373 cal., 16 g total fat (9 g sat. fat), 58 mg chol., 1,036 mg sodium, 35 g carbo., 3 g fiber, 22 g pro.
DAILY VALUES: 64% vit. A, 159% vit. C, 29% calcium, 13% iron

6 SERVINGS	INGREDIENTS	4 SERVINGS
1½ cups	dried elbow macaroni	1 cup
3 cups	broccoli florets	2 cups
1½ cups	coarsely chopped red sweet pepper	1 cup
1½ cups (8 oz.)	cubed cooked ham	1 cup (5 oz.)
1½ cups	milk	1 cup
4½ tsp.	cornstarch	1 Tbsp.
¼ tsp.	black pepper	⅛ tsp.
1½ cups (6 oz.)	cubed American cheese	1 cup (4 oz.)
1 cup	soft bread crumbs	¾ cup
1 Tbsp.	butter or margarine, melted	1 Tbsp.

CHAPTER 4

p. 122   p. 124

p. 125   p. 130

p. 132   p. 135

SELECT SEAFOOD ENTRÉES

RECIPE FINDER

FOR MORE RECIPES:

Visit our Recipe Center at www.bhg.com/bkrecipe

Crawfish Fettuccine, p.128

Asian Shrimp and Millet Salad

This orange-scented salad is divine. It uses millet, a high-protein cereal grass that tastes like rice. Look for millet in Asian markets or health food stores.

PREP: 25 minutes   CHILL: 4 to 24 hours

10 SERVINGS	INGREDIENTS	5 SERVINGS
2 cups	millet	1 cup
2 Tbsp.	cooking oil	1 Tbsp.
4 cups	water	2 cups
4 cups	cooked, peeled, and deveined shrimp (remove tails, if present)	2 cups
2	mango(es), peeled, seeded, and chopped	1
2 8-oz. cans	sliced water chestnuts, drained	1 8-oz. can
1 cup	chopped red onion	1/2 cup
1/2 cup	snipped fresh cilantro	1/4 cup
1/2 cup	rice vinegar	1/4 cup
1/2 cup	salad oil	1/4 cup
2 Tbsp.	finely shredded orange peel	1 Tbsp.
2 tsp.	toasted sesame oil	1 tsp.
1/2 tsp.	salt	1/4 tsp.

1 In a large saucepan cook and stir millet in hot cooking oil over medium heat for 2 minutes. Carefully add water. Bring to boiling; reduce heat. Simmer, covered, about 25 minutes or until millet is fluffy and water is absorbed.

2 Transfer millet to a very large bowl. Add shrimp, mangoes, water chestnuts, onion, and cilantro; toss to combine. In a screw-top jar combine vinegar, salad oil, orange peel, sesame oil, and salt. Pour over millet mixture; toss to coat. Cover and chill for 4 to 24 hours.

For 5 servings: Prepare using method above, except cook millet in a medium saucepan. Stir salad together in a large bowl.

To tote: Transport salad in an insulated cooler with ice packs.

NUTRITION FACTS PER SERVING: 377 cal., 17 g total fat (2 g sat. fat), 0 mg chol., 449 mg sodium, 44 g carbo., 6 g fiber, 14 g pro.
DAILY VALUES: 39% vit. A, 27% vit. C, 6% calcium, 11% iron

Citrus Tuna Pasta Salad

Yellow sweet peppers, artichoke hearts, ripe olives, and a light lemon-herb dressing highlight this delicious and pretty pasta salad.

1 Cook pasta in a Dutch oven according to package directions, adding the artichoke hearts for the last 5 minutes of cooking; drain. Rinse with cold water; drain again. Halve any large artichoke hearts.

2 Transfer pasta and artichoke hearts to a very large bowl. Gently stir in tuna, mushrooms, sweet peppers, and olives.

3 Pour Lemon Dressing over pasta mixture; toss to coat. Cover and chill for 4 to 24 hours. Before serving, gently stir in tomatoes and sprinkle with Parmesan cheese.

Lemon Dressing: In a small bowl whisk together 2 teaspoons finely shredded lemon peel; $^1/_3$ cup lemon juice; $^1/_3$ cup rice vinegar or white wine vinegar; $^1/_4$ cup salad oil; 2 tablespoons snipped fresh thyme or basil or 2 teaspoons dried thyme or basil, crushed; 1 teaspoon sugar; $^1/_2$ teaspoon black pepper; and 4 cloves garlic, minced. Makes about $^3/_4$ cup.

For 4 servings: Prepare using method above, except cook pasta and artichoke hearts in a large saucepan. Stir salad together in a large bowl.

To tote: Transport salad, tomatoes, and Parmesan cheese in an insulated cooler with ice packs.

NUTRITION FACTS PER SERVING: 394 cal., 12 g total fat (2 g sat. fat), 31 mg chol., 407 mg sodium, 45 g carbo., 6 g fiber, 25 g pro.
DAILY VALUES: 11% vit. A, 148% vit. C, 10% calcium, 18% iron

PREP: 30 minutes CHILL: 4 to 24 hours

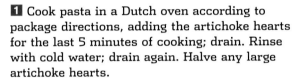

8 SERVINGS	INGREDIENTS	4 SERVINGS
12 oz.	dried mafalda	6 oz.
2 9-oz. pkgs.	frozen artichoke hearts, thawed	1 9-oz. pkg.
2 9$^1/_4$-oz. cans	chunk white tuna (water packed), drained and broken into chunks	1 9$^1/_4$-oz. can
2 cups	sliced fresh mushrooms	1 cup
2 cups	chopped yellow sweet peppers	1 cup
$^1/_2$ cup	sliced pitted ripe olives	$^1/_4$ cup
1 recipe	Lemon Dressing	$^1/_3$ cup
2 cups	cherry tomatoes, halved	1 cup
$^1/_4$ cup	finely shredded Parmesan cheese	2 Tbsp.

Fruited Tuna Salad

Vanilla yogurt and oranges partner in the luscious dressing for this colorful tuna salad, taking everyday tuna salad up a notch or two.

PREP: 35 minutes   CHILL: Up to 4 hours

INGREDIENTS

8 SERVINGS		4 SERVINGS
2 8-oz. cartons	vanilla yogurt	1 8-oz. carton
2 tsp.	finely shredded orange peel	1 tsp.
4	oranges, peeled and sectioned*	2
3 cups	cubed cantaloupe and/or honeydew melon*	1 1/2 cups
3 cups	halved strawberries	1 1/2 cups
1/4 cup	sliced green onions	2 Tbsp.
3 9-oz. cans	solid white tuna, drained and coarsely flaked	2 6-oz. cans
	Leaf lettuce (optional)	
1/2 cup	chopped pecans, toasted	1/4 cup

1 In a large bowl stir together vanilla yogurt and orange peel. Add orange sections, cantaloupe, strawberries, and green onions. Toss gently to coat. Add tuna; toss gently. Cover and chill for up to 4 hours.

2 To serve, if desired, place a lettuce leaf on each salad plate. Spoon tuna mixture onto plates; sprinkle salads with pecans.

To tote: Transport salad and nuts in an insulated cooler with ice packs. Just before serving, sprinkle with nuts.

*To save time: Omit the fresh orange sections and substitute two 11-ounce cans mandarin orange sections, drained, for the 4 oranges. (Substitute one 11-ounce can mandarin orange sections, drained, for the 2 oranges in the 4-serving version.) Buy a mixture of already cubed melon or melon balls from the deli or salad bar of your supermarket.

NUTRITION FACTS PER SERVING: 272 cal., 9 g total fat (2 g sat. fat), 43 mg chol., 405 mg sodium, 22 g carbo., 3 g fiber, 27 g pro.
DAILY VALUES: 45% vit. A, 126% vit. C, 15% calcium, 9% iron

Island-Style Seafood Slaw

Shrimp, sweet peppers, lime, and cilantro make for stellar additions. The honey-roasted peanuts add a light sweetness and crunch.

PREP: 30 minutes CHILL: Up to 2 hours

INGREDIENTS

8 SERVINGS		4 SERVINGS
2 12-oz. pkgs.	frozen peeled, cooked shrimp	1 12-oz. pkg.
12 cups	packaged shredded cabbage with carrot (coleslaw mix)	6 cups
4 medium	red and/or yellow sweet peppers, cut into thin, bite-size strips	2 medium
2/3 cup	thinly sliced green onions	1/3 cup
1/2 cup	snipped fresh cilantro	1/4 cup
1 1/2 cups	light mayonnaise dressing or salad dressing	3/4 cup
2 tsp.	finely shredded lime peel	1 tsp.
1/3 cup	lime juice	3 Tbsp.
1/2 tsp.	salt	1/4 tsp.
1/4 tsp.	ground red pepper	1/8 tsp.
1/2 cup	honey-roasted peanuts (optional)	1/4 cup

1 Thaw shrimp, if frozen. Rinse shrimp; pat dry. In a very large bowl toss together shrimp, cabbage, sweet peppers, green onions, and cilantro.

2 For dressing, in a small bowl stir together mayonnaise dressing, lime peel, lime juice, salt, and ground red pepper. Pour dressing over salad, tossing to coat. Cover and chill for up to 2 hours. If desired, sprinkle with peanuts just before serving.

To tote: Transport salad and, if desired, peanuts in an insulated cooler with ice packs.

NUTRITION FACTS PER SERVING: 295 cal., 16 g total fat (3 g sat. fat), 181 mg chol., 648 mg sodium, 21 g carbo., 5 g fiber, 20 g pro.
DAILY VALUES: 91% vit. A, 293% vit. C, 11% calcium, 17% iron

Fish Chowder

When you're hosting the potluck, bring out this chowder and you will be all the rage. It will warm you up on a chilly evening.

1 Thaw fish, if frozen. Rinse fish; pat dry. Cut fish into 2-inch pieces; cover and chill. In a 5- or 6-quart slow cooker combine potatoes, onions, celery, butter, bay leaves, salt, dill, and pepper. Stir in water and vermouth.

2 Cover; cook on high-heat setting for 3¹/₂ hours. Place fish on top of vegetable mixture. Cover and cook on high-heat setting for 30 to 45 minutes more or until fish flakes easily. Remove bay leaves. Break fish into bite-size pieces with a fork. Stir in whipping cream and parsley.

For 8 servings: Prepare using method above, except assemble in a 4- or 4¹/₂-quart slow cooker.

To tote: Transport the slow cooker in an insulated carrier.

NUTRITION FACTS PER SERVING: 450 cal., 29 g total fat (18 g sat. fat), 151 mg chol., 764 mg sodium, 19 g carbo., 2 g fiber, 25 g pro.
DAILY VALUES: 24% vit. A, 29% vit. C, 8% calcium, 8% iron

PREP: 35 minutes   COOK: 4 hours

12 SERVINGS	INGREDIENTS	8 SERVINGS
3 lb.	fresh or frozen fish fillets (such as cod, haddock, or orange roughy)	2 lb.
2 lb.	potatoes, peeled and chopped	1¹/₃ lb.
3 cups	chopped onions	2 cups
³/₄ cup	chopped celery	¹/₂ cup
¹/₃ cup	butter or margarine, cut up	¹/₄ cup
3	bay leaves	2
3 tsp.	salt	2 tsp.
³/₄ tsp.	dried dill	¹/₂ tsp.
³/₄ tsp.	black pepper	¹/₂ tsp.
3 cups	water	2 cups
³/₄ cup	dry vermouth, dry white wine, or water	¹/₂ cup
3 cups	whipping cream or evaporated milk	2 cups
¹/₃ cup	snipped fresh parsley	¹/₄ cup

Tuna-Noodle Casserole

This is not your ordinary tuna-noodle casserole. Mushrooms, green beans, and Swiss cheese add to its intrigue. You most likely won't have leftovers to take home!

PREP: 30 minutes
BAKE: 30 minutes OVEN: 350°F

12 SERVINGS — INGREDIENTS — 6 SERVINGS

12 SERVINGS	INGREDIENTS	6 SERVINGS
8 oz.	dried medium noodles	4 oz.
1 16-oz. pkg.	frozen whole or cut green beans	1 10-oz. pkg.
1/2 cup	fine dry bread crumbs	1/4 cup
2 Tbsp.	butter or margarine, melted	1 Tbsp.
2 Tbsp.	butter or margarine	1 Tbsp.
2 cups	sliced fresh mushrooms	1 cup
1 1/2 cups	chopped red or green sweet pepper	3/4 cup
1 cup	chopped onion	1/2 cup
1 cup	sliced celery	1/2 cup
2 cloves	garlic, minced	1 clove
2 10 3/4-oz. cans	condensed cream of mushroom or celery soup	1 10 3/4-oz. can
1 cup	milk	1/2 cup
1 cup (4 oz.)	shredded process Swiss or American cheese	1/2 cup (2 oz.)
2 9-oz. cans	tuna (water packed), drained and flaked	1 9-oz. can

1 Cook noodles according to package directions, adding the green beans for the last 3 minutes of cooking. Drain and set aside. Meanwhile, toss the bread crumbs with the 2 tablespoons melted butter; set aside.

2 In a 12-inch skillet melt 2 tablespoons butter over medium heat. Add mushrooms, sweet pepper, onion, celery, and garlic. Cook and stir until vegetables are tender. Add soup, milk, and cheese, stirring until cheese is melted. Stir in tuna, cooked noodles, and green beans.

3 Spoon tuna mixture into a 3-quart casserole. Sprinkle bread crumb mixture over casserole. Bake, uncovered, in a 350° oven for 30 to 35 minutes or until heated through and bread crumbs are golden.

For 6 servings: Prepare using method above, except spoon tuna mixture into a 2-quart casserole.

To tote: Cover casserole tightly. Transport in an insulated carrier.

NUTRITION FACTS PER SERVING: 306 cal., 13 g total fat (6 g sat. fat), 57 mg chol., 746 mg sodium, 28 g carbo., 3 g fiber, 19 g pro.
DAILY VALUES: 29% vit. A, 60% vit. C, 16% calcium, 12% iron

Crawfish Fettuccine

This is a great way to fix crawfish at home when it's in season. You also can make the dish with shrimp.

PREP: 25 minutes
BAKE: 20 minutes OVEN: 350°F

8 SERVINGS	INGREDIENTS	4 SERVINGS
1 lb.	fresh or frozen peeled, cooked crawfish tails*	8 oz.
1 lb.	dried fettuccine, broken	8 oz.
1 cup	coarsely chopped green sweet pepper	1/2 cup
3/4 cup	chopped onion	1/3 cup
4 cloves	garlic, minced	2 cloves
1/4 cup	butter or margarine	2 Tbsp.
3 Tbsp.	all-purpose flour	4 tsp.
1/4 to 1/2 tsp.	ground red pepper	1/8 to 1/4 tsp.
1/4 tsp.	salt	1/8 tsp.
2 cups	half-and-half, light cream, or milk	1 cup
1 1/2 cups (6 oz.)	shredded American cheese	3/4 cup (3 oz.)
2 Tbsp.	snipped fresh parsley	1 Tbsp.
1/3 cup	grated Parmesan cheese	3 Tbsp.

1 Thaw crawfish, if frozen. In a Dutch oven cook fettuccine according to package directions. Drain; return to Dutch oven.

2 Meanwhile, for sauce, in a large saucepan cook sweet pepper, onion, and garlic in hot butter about 5 minutes or until tender. Stir in flour, ground red pepper, and salt. Add half-and-half all at once. Cook and stir over medium heat until thickened and bubbly. Add American cheese, stirring until melted. Remove from heat; stir in crawfish and parsley. Pour sauce over fettuccine, tossing gently to coat. Spoon mixture into an ungreased 3-quart rectangular baking dish. Sprinkle with Parmesan cheese. Bake, covered, in a 350° oven for 20 to 25 minutes or until heated through.

For 4 servings: Prepare as above, except spoon mixture into a 2-quart square baking dish.

To tote: Transport in an insulated carrier.

*NOTE: If you aren't able to find peeled crawfish tails, purchase 4 pounds of whole, head-on crawfish for the 8-serving size or 2 pounds for the 4-serving size. These will yield 1 pound and 8 ounces respectively. Allow about 1 hour to peel crawfish.

NUTRITION FACTS PER SERVING: 506 cal., 22 g total fat (13 g sat. fat), 123 mg chol., 574 mg sodium, 51 g carbo., 2 g fiber, 25 g pro.
DAILY VALUES: 20% vit. A, 29% vit. C, 29% calcium, 13% iron

Baked Shrimp Curry

A trio of spices—curry powder, paprika, and nutmeg—uniquely flavors the cream sauce. The condiments chutney, orange peel, coconut, or peanuts supply additional flavor.

1 Thaw shrimp, if frozen. Rinse shrimp; pat dry. In a saucepan melt butter. Stir in flour, curry powder, paprika, and nutmeg. Stir in half-and-half all at once. Cook and stir over medium heat until thickened and bubbly. Cook and stir 1 minute more. Stir in shrimp, sherry (if desired), lemon juice, ginger, and Worcestershire sauce; heat through. Transfer to an ungreased 2-quart casserole.

2 Bake, uncovered, in a 400° oven about 15 minutes or until bubbly and lightly browned. Serve with rice. If desired, pass condiments to sprinkle on each serving.

For 4 servings: Prepare using method above, except transfer mixture to a 1-quart casserole.

To tote: Cover tightly. Transport casserole and hot cooked rice, separately, in an insulated carrier. If desired, transport condiments in an insulated cooler with ice packs.

NUTRITION FACTS PER SERVING: 358 cal., 15 g total fat (9 g sat. fat), 260 mg chol., 342 mg sodium, 27 g carbo., 1 g fiber, 28 g pro.
DAILY VALUES: 17% vit. A, 6% vit. C, 12% calcium, 27% iron

PREP: 30 minutes
BAKE: 15 minutes OVEN: 400°F

INGREDIENTS

8 SERVINGS		4 SERVINGS
2 lb.	fresh or frozen peeled, cooked shrimp	1 lb.
1/4 cup	butter or margarine	2 Tbsp.
2 Tbsp.	all-purpose flour	1 Tbsp.
1 Tbsp.	curry powder	1 1/2 tsp.
1/2 tsp.	paprika	1/4 tsp.
1/8 tsp.	ground nutmeg	Dash
2 cups	half-and-half, light cream, or milk	1 cup
2 Tbsp.	dry sherry (optional)	1 Tbsp.
2 tsp.	lemon juice	1 tsp.
2 tsp.	grated fresh ginger	1 tsp.
1/8 tsp.	Worcestershire sauce	Dash
4 cups	hot cooked rice	2 cups

Chutney, finely shredded orange peel, flaked coconut, and/or chopped peanuts (optional)

Cheesy Shrimp and Rice

Swiss and cheddar cheese combine with mushroom soup for this shrimp dish. Purchase deveined shrimp to keep prep time down.

PREP: 40 minutes BAKE: 35 minutes
STAND: 10 minutes OVEN: 375°F

INGREDIENTS

12 SERVINGS		6 SERVINGS
2 6.2-oz. pkgs.	quick-cooking long grain and wild rice mix	1 6.2-oz. pkg.
2 cups	chopped red sweet pepper(s)	1 cup
2 cups	chopped celery	1 cup
2 cups	chopped onions	1 cup
1/3 cup	butter or margarine	3 Tbsp.
2 10³/4-oz. cans	condensed golden mushroom soup	1 10³/4-oz. can
2 cups (8 oz.)	shredded Swiss cheese	1 cup (4 oz.)
2 cups (8 oz.)	shredded cheddar cheese	1 cup (4 oz.)
1/2 tsp.	black pepper	1/4 tsp.
2 lb.	cooked, peeled, and deveined medium shrimp (remove tails, if present)	1 lb.
	Lemon slices (optional)	

1 Prepare rice mixes according to package directions. Meanwhile, in a 4-quart Dutch oven cook and stir sweet peppers, celery, and onions in hot butter about 5 minutes or just until tender.

2 In a very large bowl combine the cooked rice, cooked vegetable mixture, soup, Swiss cheese, half of the cheddar cheese, and the black pepper. Stir in the shrimp. Spoon mixture into two 3-quart rectangular baking dishes.

3 Bake, covered, in a 375° oven about 35 minutes or until heated through, rotating baking dishes halfway through baking. Remove from oven; sprinkle with remaining cheddar cheese. Let stand 10 minutes before serving (if toting, see below). If desired, garnish with lemon slices.

For 6 servings: Prepare using method above, except use a large saucepan for cooking the vegetables and spoon shrimp mixture into one 3-quart rectangular baking dish.

To tote: Do not let stand after baking. Cover tightly. Transport in an insulated carrier.

NUTRITION FACTS PER SERVING: 452 cal., 20 g total fat (11 g sat. fat), 205 mg chol., 1,274 mg sodium, 32 g carbo., 2 g fiber, 35 g pro.
DAILY VALUES: 48% vit. A, 76% vit. C, 38% calcium, 22% iron

Lobster Lasagna

Lobster, Brie cheese, and asparagus combine for this very sophisticated lasagna.

PREP: 45 minutes BAKE: 25 minutes
STAND: 5 minutes OVEN: 475°F/400°F

12 SERVINGS — INGREDIENTS — 6 SERVINGS

12 SERVINGS	INGREDIENTS	6 SERVINGS
2 lb.	fresh asparagus spears, cut into 2-inch pieces	1 lb.
2 Tbsp.	olive oil	1 Tbsp.
1 9-oz. pkg.	no-boil lasagna noodles	1/2 9-oz. pkg.
1/4 cup	butter or margarine	2 Tbsp.
1/4 cup	all-purpose flour	2 Tbsp.
1 1/2 cups	chicken broth	3/4 cup
1/4 tsp.	white pepper	1/8 tsp.
2 4 1/2-oz. rounds	Brie cheese, peeled and cubed	1 4 1/2-oz. round
1/4 cup	dry sherry (optional)	2 Tbsp.
2 1/2 cups	chopped cooked lobster meat, OR	1 1/4 cups
2 6- or 8-oz. pkgs.	flake-style imitation lobster	1 6- or 8-oz. pkg.
2/3 cup	finely shredded Parmesan cheese	1/3 cup
1 cup	chopped tomato	1/2 cup

1 Grease a 3-quart rectangular baking dish; set aside. Place asparagus in a 13×9×2-inch baking pan; toss with oil. Bake, uncovered, in a 475° oven for 5 to 8 minutes or until crisp-tender; cool.

2 Meanwhile, soak lasagna noodles in water for 15 minutes; drain. Reduce oven temperature to 400°.

3 For sauce, in a small saucepan melt butter over medium heat; stir in flour. Cook and stir for 5 minutes or until flour mixture is light brown. Stir in broth and pepper. Cook and stir until bubbly. Reduce heat to low. Stir in Brie until almost melted. If desired, stir in sherry. Place one-third of lasagna noodles in the bottom of prepared dish, overlapping or trimming as necessary to fit. Top with 1/3 cup of sauce, half of asparagus, and half of lobster. Sprinkle with one-third of the Parmesan cheese.

4 Repeat layers with another one-third of the noodles, 1/3 cup of sauce, remaining asparagus, remaining lobster, and another one-third of the cheese. Top with remaining lasagna noodles, tomato, remaining sauce, and Parmesan cheese.

5 Bake, covered, in the 400° oven for 20 minutes. Uncover; bake for 5 to 10 minutes more or until bubbly. Let stand 5 minutes before serving (if toting, see below).

For 6 servings: Prepare using method above, except assemble and bake in a 2-quart square baking dish.

To tote: Do not let stand after baking. Cover tightly. Transport in an insulated carrier.

NUTRITION FACTS PER SERVING: 283 cal., 15 g total fat (8 g sat. fat), 67 mg chol., 438 mg sodium, 19 g carbo., 1 g fiber, 18 g pro.
DAILY VALUES: 11% vit. A, 21% vit. C, 12% calcium, 7% iron

Lobster Rolls

Lobster for a potluck? Why not? Frozen lobster takes less time to cook than many meats. Of course, you'll want to reserve these sandwiches for only the most important celebrations!

1 Thaw lobster tails, if frozen. In a large saucepan cook lobster tails, uncovered, in boiling water for 8 to 12 minutes or until shells turn bright red and meat is tender; drain. (Cook lobster half at a time, if necessary.) Let stand about 20 minutes or until cool enough to handle. Remove and discard shells. Coarsely chop meat (you should have about 4 cups).

2 In a medium bowl combine lobster meat, mayonnaise, green onions, sweet pepper, lemon peel, lemon juice, and hot pepper sauce. Cover and chill for 1 hour.

3 Hollow out the bottom half of each baguette, leaving a thick shell. Line the bottom of each baguette with a romaine leaf; spoon lobster mixture on top of romaine. Place top half of baguette on lobster mixture.

To tote: Wrap each lobster roll in plastic wrap. Transport in an insulated cooler with ice packs. Serve within 2 hours.

NUTRITION FACTS PER SERVING: 575 cal., 19 g total fat (3 g sat. fat), 62 mg chol., 1,197 mg sodium, 73 g carbo., 5 g fiber, 27 g pro.
DAILY VALUES: 9% vit. A, 15% vit. C, 16% calcium, 22% iron

PREP: 20 minutes
STAND: 20 minutes   CHILL: 1 hour

8 SERVINGS	INGREDIENTS	4 SERVINGS
4 8-oz.	fresh or frozen lobster tails	2 8-oz.
2/3 cup	mayonnaise or salad dressing	1/3 cup
4	green onions, thinly sliced	2
2 Tbsp.	finely chopped red sweet pepper	1 Tbsp.
2 tsp.	finely shredded lemon peel	1 tsp.
2 tsp.	lemon juice	1 tsp.
Several drops	bottled hot pepper sauce	Few drops
8 6-inch pieces	baguette-style French bread, halved lengthwise, OR	4 6-inch pieces
8	hoagie buns, split	4
8	romaine leaves	4

Seafood Rice Casserole

This hearty casserole features shrimp, imitation crabmeat, rice, and vegetables. It's perfect party food.

1 Thaw shrimp, if frozen. Rinse shrimp; pat dry. In a large skillet cook mushrooms, onion, and sweet pepper in hot oil over medium heat about 5 minutes or until tender. In a very large bowl stir together cooked vegetables, cooked rice, water chestnuts, mayonnaise, tomato juice, salt, and pepper; mix well. Stir in shrimp and imitation crabmeat.

2 Spoon seafood mixture into an ungreased 2-quart rectangular baking dish. Bake, covered, in a 350° oven for 30 to 35 minutes or until bubbly. Just before serving, sprinkle with almonds.

For 4 servings: Prepare using method above, except spoon seafood mixture into a 1^{1}/$_{2}$-quart round casserole dish.

To tote: Cover tightly. Transport casserole and almonds in an insulated carrier.

NUTRITION FACTS PER SERVING: 419 cal., 30 g total fat (4 g sat. fat), 103 mg chol., 618 mg sodium, 24 g carbo., 2 g fiber, 17 g pro.
DAILY VALUES: 8% vit. A, 25% vit. C, 6% calcium, 17% iron

PREP: 30 minutes
BAKE: 30 minutes   OVEN: 350°F

INGREDIENTS

8 SERVINGS		4 SERVINGS
1 12-oz. pkg.	frozen peeled, cooked shrimp	6 oz.
3 cups	sliced fresh mushrooms	1^{1}/$_{2}$ cups
1 small	onion, cut into thin wedges	1/2 small
1/2 cup	chopped green sweet pepper	1/4 cup
1 Tbsp.	cooking oil	2 tsp.
2^{1}/$_{2}$ cups	cooked white rice	1^{1}/$_{4}$ cups
1 8-oz. can	sliced water chestnuts, drained	1/2 8-oz. can (1/2 cup)
1 cup	mayonnaise or salad dressing	1/2 cup
1 cup	tomato juice	1/2 cup
1/4 tsp.	salt	1/8 tsp.
1/8 tsp.	black pepper	Dash
1 6- or 8-oz. pkg.	flake-style imitation crabmeat	1/2 6- or 8-oz. pkg. (1/2 cup)
1/2 cup	sliced almonds, toasted	1/4 cup

CHAPTER 5

ESSENTIAL SIDES

RECIPE FINDER

p. 139 p. 143

p. 146 p. 150

p. 153 p. 154

FOR MORE RECIPES:

Visit our Recipe Center at www.bhg.com/bkrecipe

Fresh Vegetable Gratin, p.154

Cranberry-Broccoli Salad

This salad is a good holiday dish. Because cranberries freeze so well, you can make it year-round. No frozen cranberries? Omit the sugar and use dried cranberries instead.

PREP: 20 minutes   CHILL: 2 to 24 hours

10 SERVINGS	INGREDIENTS	5 SERVINGS
1¹/₄ cups	cranberries, chopped	²/₃ cup
¹/₄ cup	sugar	2 Tbsp.
4 cups	broccoli florets	2 cups
4 cups	packaged shredded cabbage with carrot (coleslaw mix)	2 cups
¹/₂ cup	chopped walnuts	¹/₄ cup
¹/₂ cup	raisins	¹/₄ cup
¹/₃ cup	chopped onion	3 Tbsp.
6 slices	bacon, crisp-cooked, drained, and crumbled	3 slices
1 cup	light mayonnaise dressing or mayonnaise	¹/₂ cup
¹/₄ cup	sugar	2 Tbsp.
1 Tbsp.	vinegar	1¹/₂ tsp.

1 In a small bowl combine the chopped cranberries and ¹/₄ cup sugar. Cover and chill until serving time (berries will release juice).

2 In a very large bowl combine broccoli, cabbage, walnuts, raisins, onion, and bacon.

3 In another small bowl stir together the mayonnaise dressing, ¹/₄ cup sugar, and vinegar. Drizzle over broccoli mixture; toss gently to coat. Cover and chill for 2 to 24 hours.

4 Just before serving, gently fold cranberry mixture into salad.

To tote: Transport salad in an insulated cooler with ice packs.

NUTRITION FACTS PER SERVING: 229 cal., 14 g total fat (3 g sat. fat), 11 mg chol., 225 mg sodium, 26 g carbo., 3 g fiber, 4 g pro.
DAILY VALUES: 14% vit. A, 83% vit. C, 5% calcium, 4% iron

Garden and Grain Salad

This basmati rice and lentil salad is dressed with a lemony Dijon Dressing. Feta cheese, although optional, complements the lemon flavor perfectly.

1 In a medium saucepan bring water and salt to boiling; stir in lentils. Return to boiling; reduce heat. Simmer, covered, about 25 minutes or until lentils are tender but not soft. Drain well. Spoon lentils into a very large bowl; set aside.

2 Meanwhile, cook rice according to package directions. Add rice to lentils in bowl. Set lentils and rice aside for about 20 minutes or until cool.

3 Gently stir sweet pepper, carrots, celery, cucumber, radishes, and green onions into cooled lentil-rice mixture. Add Dijon Dressing; toss gently to coat. Cover and chill for 4 to 24 hours. If desired, sprinkle with feta cheese.

Dijon Dressing: In a blender container combine $^3/_4$ cup olive oil, $^1/_3$ cup lemon juice, $^1/_3$ cup Dijon-style mustard, $^1/_2$ teaspoon salt, $^1/_4$ teaspoon black pepper, and 2 cloves garlic, minced. Cover and blend until smooth. Makes about $1^1/_2$ cups.

To tote: Transport salad and, if desired, feta cheese in an insulated cooler with ice packs.

NUTRITION FACTS PER SERVING: 190 cal., 11 g total fat (1 g sat. fat), 0 mg chol., 186 mg sodium, 20 g carbo., 5 g fiber, 5 g pro.
DAILY VALUES: 54% vit. A, 47% vit. C, 3% calcium, 10% iron

PREP: 40 minutes
COOL: 20 minutes   CHILL: 4 to 24 hours

16 SERVINGS	INGREDIENTS	8 SERVINGS
4 cups	water	2 cups
$^1/_2$ tsp.	salt	$^1/_4$ tsp.
1 cup	brown lentils, rinsed and drained	$^1/_2$ cup
1 cup	uncooked basmati rice or long grain rice	$^1/_2$ cup
$1^1/_2$ cups	coarsely chopped red, yellow, and/or green sweet pepper	$^3/_4$ cup
1 cup	chopped carrots	$^1/_2$ cup
1 cup	sliced celery	$^1/_2$ cup
$^1/_2$ cup	chopped seedless cucumber	$^1/_4$ cup
$^1/_2$ cup	chopped radishes	$^1/_4$ cup
$^1/_2$ cup	chopped green onions	$^1/_4$ cup
1 recipe	Dijon Dressing	$^3/_4$ cup
1 cup (4 oz.)	crumbled feta cheese (optional)	$^1/_2$ cup (2 oz.)

Minted Wild Rice Salad

Beautiful and tasty, this salad is one you'll be asked for again and again. Mint provides a refreshing flavor.

PREP: 20 minutes
COOK: 40 minutes   CHILL: 2 to 8 hours

INGREDIENTS

12 SERVINGS		6 SERVINGS
1 cup	uncooked wild rice, rinsed and drained	1/2 cup
1 1/2 cups	chopped tomatoes	3/4 cup
1 cup	chopped yellow, green, or red sweet pepper	1/2 cup
1 cup	chopped green onions	1/2 cup
2/3 cup	golden raisins or dried cherries	1/3 cup
2/3 cup	chopped pecans, toasted	1/3 cup
1/2 cup	snipped fresh mint	1/4 cup
1/3 cup	olive oil	3 Tbsp.
1/3 cup	lemon juice	3 Tbsp.
1/2 tsp.	salt	1/4 tsp.
1/2 tsp.	black pepper	1/4 tsp.

1 Cook wild rice according to package directions; drain and cool.

2 In a large bowl combine cooled rice, tomatoes, sweet pepper, green onions, raisins, pecans, and mint; set aside.

3 In a small bowl combine oil, lemon juice, salt, and pepper; mix well. Pour over wild rice mixture, tossing to coat. Cover; chill for 2 to 8 hours.

To tote: Transport salad in an insulated cooler with ice packs.

NUTRITION FACTS PER SERVING: 184 cal., 11 g total fat (1 g sat. fat), 0 mg chol., 105 mg sodium, 21 g carbo., 3 g fiber, 3 g pro.
DAILY VALUES: 8% vit. A, 35% vit. C, 3% calcium, 8% iron

Garlic Roasted Vegetable Salad

New potatoes, green beans, garlic, rosemary, and balsamic vinegar combine for a vegetable salad you'll crave after the bowl is licked clean.

PREP: 20 minutes
ROAST: 1 hour OVEN: 400°F

INGREDIENTS

8 SERVINGS		4 SERVINGS
8 oz.	green beans, cut into 1¹/₂-inch pieces	4 oz.
1 head	garlic	1 head
2 lb.	tiny new potatoes, quartered	1 lb.
2 medium	red sweet pepper(s), cut into large chunks	1 medium
4	green onions, sliced	2
	Salt and black pepper	
¹/₄ cup	chicken broth	2 Tbsp.
¹/₄ cup	balsamic vinegar	2 Tbsp.
2 Tbsp.	olive oil	1 Tbsp.
1 tsp.	snipped fresh rosemary	¹/₂ tsp.

1 Cook green beans in boiling water for 3 minutes. Drain; place in ice water to cool. Drain beans again; set aside.

2 Peel away the dry outer layers of skin from the head of garlic, leaving skins and cloves intact. Cut off the pointed top portion (about ¹/₄ inch), leaving bulb intact but exposing tops of individual cloves.

3 Place the garlic head, cut side up, in a shallow roasting pan. Add green beans, potatoes, sweet peppers, and green onions. Sprinkle with salt and black pepper. Drizzle chicken broth over all. Roast, uncovered, in a 400° oven about 1 hour. Cool slightly.

4 For dressing, squeeze out the garlic paste from individual cloves into a bowl; add vinegar, olive oil, and rosemary. Stir to combine. Transfer roasted vegetables to a bowl. Add dressing; toss to coat. Serve warm, or cover and chill for 4 to 6 hours.

For 4 servings: Prepare as above, except add only half of the roasted head of garlic to the dressing. Cover and chill remaining garlic for another use.

To tote: Cover warm salad tightly. Transport warm salad in an insulated carrier. Transport chilled salad in an insulated cooler with ice packs.

NUTRITION FACTS PER SERVING: 143 cal., 4 g total fat (1 g sat. fat), 0 mg chol., 43 mg sodium, 25 g carbo., 4 g fiber, 4 g pro.
DAILY VALUES: 36% vit. A, 115% vit. C, 4% calcium, 12% iron

Sweet Potato Salad

A sweet potato salad will stand out on any potluck party table. Orange, ginger, honey, and nutmeg all flavor the dressing.

1 In a Dutch oven combine sweet potatoes, salt (if desired), and enough water to cover. Bring to boiling; reduce heat. Simmer, covered, about 15 minutes or just until potatoes are tender. Drain well and cool slightly.

2 Meanwhile, for dressing, in a very large bowl combine mayonnaise dressing, orange peel, orange juice, honey, ginger, and nutmeg. Stir in celery and apricots. Add cooked potatoes; toss lightly to coat. Cover and chill for 8 to 24 hours.

3 Just before serving, stir in nuts and pineapple.

For 8 servings: Prepare as above, except combine salad ingredients in a large bowl.

To tote: Transport salad, nuts, and pineapple in an insulated cooler with ice packs.

NUTRITION FACTS PER SERVING: 270 cal., 15 g total fat (3 g sat. fat), 10 mg chol., 204 mg sodium, 34 g carbo., 4 g fiber, 3 g pro.
DAILY VALUES: 302% vit. A, 35% vit. C, 4% calcium, 6% iron

PREP: 40 minutes   CHILL: 8 to 24 hours

16 SERVINGS	INGREDIENTS	8 SERVINGS
4 lb.	sweet potatoes, peeled and cubed	2 lb.
1/4 tsp.	salt (optional)	1/8 tsp.
2 cups	light mayonnaise dressing or salad dressing	1 cup
2 Tbsp.	finely shredded orange peel	1 Tbsp.
2/3 cup	orange juice	1/3 cup
2 Tbsp.	honey	1 Tbsp.
1/2 tsp.	grated fresh ginger OR	1/4 tsp.
1/8 tsp.	ground ginger	Dash
1/4 tsp.	ground nutmeg	1/8 tsp.
2 cups	sliced celery	1 cup
1/2 cup	snipped dried apricots	1/4 cup
1 cup	chopped walnuts or pecans, toasted	1/2 cup
1 cup	canned pineapple tidbits, drained	1/2 cup

Marinated Vegetable Salad

This vegetable salad can be refrigerated for up to 24 hours, making it a blessing when you don't have time to prepare the salad the day of your picnic, party, or potluck.

PREP: 20 minutes STAND: 30 minutes

12 SERVINGS	INGREDIENTS	6 SERVINGS
4 medium	tomatoes OR	2 medium
8	roma tomatoes, cut into wedges	4
2 medium	green sweet pepper(s), cut into small squares	1 medium
2 1/2 cups	thinly sliced zucchini or yellow summer squash	1 1/4 cups
1/2 cup	thinly sliced red onion	1/4 cup
1/4 cup	snipped fresh parsley	2 Tbsp.
1/4 cup	olive oil	2 Tbsp.
1/4 cup	balsamic or wine vinegar	2 Tbsp.
1/4 cup	water	2 Tbsp.
2 Tbsp.	snipped fresh thyme or basil OR	1 Tbsp.
1 tsp.	dried thyme or basil, crushed	1 tsp.
2 cloves	garlic, minced	1 clove

1 In a large bowl combine tomatoes, sweet peppers, zucchini, onion, and parsley; set aside.

2 For dressing, in a screw-top jar combine oil, vinegar, water, thyme, and garlic. Cover and shake well. Pour dressing over vegetable mixture. Toss lightly to coat.

3 Let vegetable mixture stand at room temperature for 30 to 60 minutes, stirring occasionally. (Or cover and chill for 4 to 24 hours, stirring once or twice. Let stand at room temperature about 30 minutes before serving.) Serve with a slotted spoon.

To tote: Cover room temperature salad tightly. Transport in an insulated carrier. Transport chilled salad in an insulated cooler with ice packs.

NUTRITION FACTS PER SERVING: 64 cal., 5 g total fat (1 g sat. fat), 0 mg chol., 6 mg sodium, 5 g carbo., 1 g fiber, 1 g pro.
DAILY VALUES: 11% vit. A, 51% vit. C, 1% calcium, 3% iron

Broccoli-Cauliflower Salad

Straightforward and delicious, this broccoli and cauliflower salad is a classic dish that is hard to resist. A little horseradish and lemon add zip to the mayonnaise dressing.

PREP: 20 minutes   CHILL: 4 to 24 hours

INGREDIENTS

8 SERVINGS		4 SERVINGS
4 cups	small cauliflower florets	2 cups
3 cups	small broccoli florets	1 1/2 cups
4	green onions, thinly sliced	2
3/4 cup	sliced radishes	1/3 cup
1/2 cup	shredded carrot	1/4 cup
1 cup	mayonnaise or salad dressing	1/2 cup
2 Tbsp.	sugar	1 Tbsp.
1 Tbsp.	lemon juice	1 1/2 tsp.
2 tsp.	prepared horseradish	1 tsp.
1/2 tsp.	salt	1/4 tsp.
1/2 tsp.	black pepper	1/4 tsp.
6 slices	bacon, crisp-cooked, drained, and crumbled	3 slices

1 In a large bowl layer cauliflower, broccoli, green onions, radishes, and carrot; set aside.

2 In a small bowl stir together mayonnaise, sugar, lemon juice, horseradish, salt, and pepper; spread over vegetables. Sprinkle with bacon. Cover and chill for 4 to 24 hours. Before serving, toss to coat vegetables.

For 4 servings: Prepare as above, except assemble salad in a medium bowl.

To tote: Transport salad in an insulated cooler with ice packs.

NUTRITION FACTS PER SERVING: 267 cal., 25 g total fat (4 g sat. fat), 20 mg chol., 409 mg sodium, 10 g carbo., 3 g fiber, 4 g pro.
DAILY VALUES: 51% vit. A, 99% vit. C, 4% calcium, 5% iron

Italian Basil, Tomato, and Pasta Salad

This recipes uses lots of basil. Make this salad when basil is in full supply in the summer.

1 For dressing, in a small bowl whisk together vinegar, mustard, pepper, and garlic. Gradually whisk in oil. Stir in the slivered basil. Set aside.

2 Cook pasta according to package directions; drain. Rinse with cold water; drain again.

3 Meanwhile, in a large saucepan cook frozen beans according to package directions; drain. Rinse with cold water; drain again.

4 Toss one-third of the dressing with the cooked pasta; place pasta in the bottom of a very large salad bowl. Layer ingredients on top of the pasta in the following order: cooked green beans, tomatoes, and olives. Top with remaining dressing. Sprinkle with the basil leaves, the Parmesan cheese, and parsley. Cover and chill for 4 to 24 hours. To serve, toss lightly to combine.

For 8 servings: Prepare as above, except assemble salad in a large salad bowl.

To tote: Transport salad in an insulated cooler with ice packs.

NUTRITION FACTS PER SERVING: 173 cal., 10 g total fat (2 g sat. fat), 5 mg chol., 167 mg sodium, 17 g carbo., 3 g fiber, 5 g pro.
DAILY VALUES: 16% vit. A, 26% vit. C, 8% calcium, 7% iron

PREP: 45 minutes   CHILL: 4 to 24 hours

16 SERVINGS	INGREDIENTS	8 SERVINGS
$^1/_2$ cup	red wine vinegar	$^1/_4$ cup
2 Tbsp.	Dijon-style mustard	1 Tbsp.
$^1/_4$ tsp.	black pepper	$^1/_8$ tsp.
2 cloves	garlic, minced	1 clove
$^1/_2$ cup	olive oil	$^1/_4$ cup
$^1/_2$ cup	slivered fresh basil	$^1/_4$ cup
8 oz.	dried pasta (such as rotini, bow ties, cavatelli, or penne)	4 oz.
2 9-oz. pkgs.	frozen cut green beans	1 9-oz. pkg.
6 medium	tomatoes, cut into thin wedges	3 medium
1 cup	sliced pitted kalamata olives or ripe olives	$^1/_2$ cup
2 cups	loosely packed fresh basil leaves	1 cup
$^3/_4$ cup (3 oz.)	finely shredded Parmesan cheese	$^1/_3$ cup (1$^1/_2$ oz.)

Swiss Vegetable Medley

Frozen vegetables are lifesavers in this quick-to-make side dish. Choose the mixture of vegetables you like best.

PREP: 15 minutes
BAKE: 35 minutes OVEN: 350°F

12 SERVINGS	INGREDIENTS	6 SERVINGS
2 16-oz. pkgs.	loose-pack frozen broccoli, cauliflower, and carrots, thawed	1 16-oz. pkg.
2 10³/₄-oz. cans	condensed cream of mushroom soup	1 10³/₄-oz. can
2 cups (8 oz.)	shredded Swiss cheese	1 cup (4 oz.)
²/₃ cup	dairy sour cream	¹/₃ cup
¹/₂ tsp.	black pepper	¹/₄ tsp.
2 2.8-oz. cans	French fried onions	1 2.8-oz. can

1 In a large bowl combine the thawed vegetables, soup, half of the Swiss cheese, the sour cream, and pepper. Stir in half of the French fried onions. Spoon vegetable mixture into a 3-quart rectangular baking dish.

2 Bake, covered, in a 350° oven for 30 minutes. Uncover; sprinkle with remaining cheese and French fried onions. Bake about 5 minutes more or until heated through.

For 6 servings: Prepare using method above, except spoon vegetable mixture into a 2-quart square baking dish.

To tote: Cover baking dish tightly. Transport in an insulated carrier.

NUTRITION FACTS PER SERVING: 249 cal., 17 g total fat (6 g sat. fat), 22 mg chol., 589 mg sodium, 14 g carbo., 3 g fiber, 9 g pro.
DAILY VALUES: 36% vit. A, 32% vit. C, 22% calcium, 3% iron

Best-Ever Potatoes

Two kinds of cheese, sour cream, and tomatoes make these potatoes winners for any potluck.

PREP: 25 minutes
BAKE: 30 minutes   OVEN: 350°F

INGREDIENTS

10 SERVINGS		5 SERVINGS
7 cups	coarsely chopped small red potatoes	3¹/₂ cups
1 cup	chopped onion	¹/₂ cup
1 8-oz. carton	dairy sour cream	¹/₂ cup
1 cup (4 oz.)	shredded Monterey Jack cheese	¹/₂ cup (2 oz.)
1 cup (4 oz.)	shredded sharp cheddar cheese	¹/₂ cup (2 oz.)
¹/₂ tsp.	salt	¹/₄ tsp.
¹/₄ to ¹/₂ tsp.	ground red pepper	¹/₈ to ¹/₄ tsp.
2 medium	tomato(es), seeded and chopped	1 medium

1 In a large saucepan cook potatoes and chopped onion, covered, in a small amount of boiling water for 12 to 15 minutes or until tender; drain. Stir in sour cream, Monterey Jack cheese, cheddar cheese, salt, and red pepper. Stir in chopped tomatoes. Spoon into a 2-quart rectangular baking dish. Bake, uncovered, in a 350° oven about 30 minutes or until heated through.

For 5 servings: Prepare using method above, except spoon into a 1-quart casserole.

To tote: Cover tightly. Transport baking dish in an insulated carrier.

NUTRITION FACTS PER SERVING: 214 cal., 12 g total fat (8 g sat. fat), 32 mg chol., 268 mg sodium, 19 g carbo., 2 g fiber, 9 g pro.
DAILY VALUES: 12% vit. A, 29% vit. C, 21% calcium, 8% iron

Sweet Potato Casserole

If you love sweet potatoes, you'll enjoy this dish. Take it along to your next holiday gathering at Grandma's house. The pecan topper is wonderful!

1 In a large bowl stir together the eggs, granulated sugar, melted butter, vanilla, and salt. Stir in the cooked sweet potatoes and raisins. Spread sweet potato mixture evenly in an ungreased 2-quart square baking dish.

2 For topping, in a small bowl combine brown sugar and flour. Using a pastry blender, cut in the cold butter until mixture resembles coarse crumbs; stir in pecans. Sprinkle over sweet potato mixture. Bake, uncovered, in a 350° oven for 35 to 40 minutes or until heated through.

For 4 servings: Prepare using method above, except spread sweet potato mixture in a 1-quart casserole.

To tote: Cover casserole tightly. Transport in an insulated carrier.

NUTRITION FACTS PER SERVING: 460 cal., 16 g total fat (7 g sat. fat), 78 mg chol., 282 mg sodium, 77 g carbo., 4 g fiber, 6 g pro.
DAILY VALUES: 574% vit. A, 48% vit. C, 7% calcium, 11% iron

PREP: 20 minutes
BAKE: 35 minutes   OVEN: 350°F

8 SERVINGS	INGREDIENTS	4 SERVINGS
2	beaten egg(s)	1
1/2 cup	granulated sugar	1/4 cup
1/4 cup	butter or margarine, melted and cooled slightly	2 Tbsp.
1 tsp.	vanilla	1/2 tsp.
1/2 tsp.	salt	1/4 tsp.
4 cups	cooked, mashed sweet potatoes	2 cups
1/2 cup	raisins	1/4 cup
1/2 cup	packed brown sugar	1/4 cup
1/4 cup	all-purpose flour	2 Tbsp.
2 Tbsp.	cold butter	1 Tbsp.
1/2 cup	chopped pecans	1/4 cup

Au Gratin Potatoes and Peas

Dill, cheddar cheese, and pimiento flavor this great-tasting potato dish. A cracker crumb topper adds the right crunch.

1 In a large saucepan combine potatoes and enough water to cover. Bring to boiling. Cook, covered, for 3 minutes. Drain; set aside.

2 Meanwhile, grease a 3-quart rectangular baking dish; set aside. In a small bowl combine the crushed crackers and the melted butter; set aside.

3 For sauce, in a large saucepan melt the 1/3 cup butter. Stir in flour, dill, salt, and pepper. Add milk all at once. Cook and stir over medium heat until thickened and bubbly. Remove from heat. Add cheese, stirring until melted.

4 Combine potatoes, peas, and pimientos in prepared baking dish; pour sauce over all. Sprinkle with cracker mixture. Bake, uncovered, in a 350° oven about 30 minutes or until potatoes are tender.

For 6 servings: Prepare as above, except use a medium saucepan for the sauce and assemble and bake in a 2-quart rectangular baking dish.

To tote: Cover tightly. Transport baking dish in an insulated carrier.

NUTRITION FACTS PER SERVING: 322 cal., 18 g total fat (10 g sat. fat), 46 mg chol., 523 mg sodium, 30 g carbo., 4 g fiber, 11 g pro.
DAILY VALUES: 27% vit. A, 47% vit. C, 23% calcium, 12% iron

PREP: 35 minutes
BAKE: 30 minutes   OVEN: 350°F

10 SERVINGS	INGREDIENTS	6 SERVINGS
1 1/2 lb.	potatoes, peeled and cut into 1/2-inch cubes	1 lb.
1 cup	coarsely crushed rich round crackers or shredded wheat wafers	1/2 cup
2 Tbsp.	butter or margarine, melted	1 Tbsp.
1/3 cup	butter or margarine	1/4 cup
1/3 cup	all-purpose flour	1/4 cup
1 tsp.	dried dill	3/4 tsp.
3/4 tsp.	salt	1/2 tsp.
1/4 tsp.	black pepper	1/8 tsp.
2 1/2 cups	milk	1 3/4 cups
1 1/2 cups (6 oz.)	shredded sharp cheddar cheese	1 cup (4 oz.)
1 16-oz. pkg.	frozen peas, thawed	1 10-oz. pkg.
1 4-oz. jar	diced pimientos, drained	1 2-oz. jar

Fresh Vegetable Gratin

A gratin is a casserole that's topped with bread crumbs or cheese. Leeks, zucchini, and yellow summer squash create a delicious and healthful side dish.

PREP: 15 minutes
BAKE: 20 minutes OVEN: 425°F

8 SERVINGS	INGREDIENTS	4 SERVINGS
4 large (2 cups)	leeks, trimmed and cut into ¹/₄-inch slices	2 large (1 cup)
2 medium (2¹/₂ cups)	zucchini, cut into ¹/₄-inch slices	1 medium (1¹/₄ cups)
2 medium (2¹/₂ cups)	yellow summer squash, cut into ¹/₄-inch slices	1 medium (1¹/₄ cups)
¹/₄ cup	olive oil	2 Tbsp.
	Salt and black pepper	
¹/₂ cup	fine dry bread crumbs	¹/₄ cup
¹/₂ cup	finely shredded Parmesan cheese	¹/₄ cup
1 tsp.	dried thyme, crushed	¹/₂ tsp.
2 cloves	garlic, minced	1 clove

1 In a medium bowl combine leeks, zucchini, yellow squash, and 2 tablespoons of the oil. Sprinkle with salt and pepper. Transfer vegetables to an ungreased 2-quart square baking dish.

2 In a small bowl stir together bread crumbs, Parmesan cheese, thyme, garlic, and remaining oil. Sprinkle crumb mixture evenly over vegetables. Bake, uncovered, in a 425° oven for 20 to 25 minutes or until vegetables are tender.

Test Kitchen Tip: Unlike green onions, the long green tops of leeks are not tender and not recommended for cooking. To trim a leek, cut off and discard these green tops. Trim off roots from the white stalk. Remove and discard any outer layers of the white stalk that appear tough. Rinse the stalk to remove any dirt or sand. Slice the stalk crosswise. (If you notice bits of dirt between the white layers, rinse again.)

To tote: Cover baking dish tightly. Transport in an insulated carrier.

NUTRITION FACTS PER SERVING: 144 cal., 9 g total fat (2 g sat. fat), 6 mg chol., 134 mg sodium, 11 g carbo., 2 g fiber, 5 g pro.
DAILY VALUES: 7% vit. A, 17% vit. C, 10% calcium, 7% iron

Fettuccine Vegetable Toss

For a pretty presentation, use spinach fettuccine and both red and yellow tomatoes. The addition of tangy feta cheese makes this a dish you'll want to serve again and again.

1 Cook fettuccine according to package directions; drain. Rinse with cold water; drain again. Transfer fettuccine to a large serving bowl; toss with half of the olive oil.

2 Meanwhile, in a large skillet heat the remaining olive oil over medium heat. Add green onions; cook and stir 30 seconds. Stir in fresh tomatoes, carrot, and dried tomatoes. Cover and cook for 5 minutes, stirring once. Spoon tomato mixture and feta cheese over cooked fettuccine; toss gently. Cover and chill for 4 to 24 hours.

To tote: Transport dish in an insulated cooler with ice packs.

NUTRITION FACTS PER SERVING: 179 cal., 6 g total fat (2 g sat. fat), 8 mg chol., 124 mg sodium, 25 g carbo., 1 g fiber, 6 g pro.
DAILY VALUES: 46% vit. A, 22% vit. C, 7% calcium, 6% iron

PREP: 20 minutes   CHILL: 4 to 24 hours

8 SERVINGS — INGREDIENTS — 4 SERVINGS

8 SERVINGS	INGREDIENTS	4 SERVINGS
8 oz.	dried spinach fettuccine or plain fettuccine	4 oz.
2 Tbsp.	olive oil	1 Tbsp.
1/4 cup	chopped green onions	2 Tbsp.
2 cups	chopped red and/or yellow tomatoes	1 cup
1/2 cup	finely chopped carrot	1/4 cup
1/4 cup	oil-packed dried tomatoes, drained and snipped	2 Tbsp.
2/3 cup	crumbled garlic-and-herb, peppercorn, or plain feta cheese	1/3 cup

CHAPTER 6

p. 166   p. 170

p. 173   p. 175

p. 178   p. 180

MOST-REQUESTED DESSERTS

RECIPE FINDER

FOR MORE RECIPES:
Visit our Recipe Center at www.bhg.com/bkdesserts

Peach of a Crumble, p.167

Peachy-Keen Upside-Down Cake

This colorful dessert starts with a packaged cake mix. Fresh peaches are best if they are in season. If not, frozen unsweetened peaches can be substituted.

PREP: 40 minutes
BAKE: 30 minutes   OVEN: 350°F

16 SERVINGS	INGREDIENTS	8 SERVINGS
1 pkg. 2-layer size	yellow cake mix	1 pkg. 1-layer size
1/2 cup	butter	1/4 cup
1 cup	packed brown sugar	1/2 cup
1 1/2 cups	sliced, peeled peaches or frozen unsweetened peach slices	3/4 cup
1/2 cup	pecan halves (optional)	1/4 cup
12	halved maraschino cherries (optional)	6

1 Prepare cake batter according to package directions; set cake batter aside.

2 Divide the butter between two 9×1 1/2-inch round cake pans. Place pans in a 350° oven about 5 minutes or until butter is melted. Remove pans from oven.

3 Stir half of the brown sugar into the butter in each pan and spread evenly over bottoms of cake pans. Arrange peach slices over brown sugar mixture. If desired, arrange pecan halves and/or cherries in spaces between peach slices. Spoon cake batter over fruit, dividing evenly.

4 Bake in the 350° oven for 30 to 35 minutes or until a wooden toothpick inserted near centers comes out clean. Cool in pan on a wire rack for 5 minutes. Loosen sides; invert onto serving plates. Serve warm.

For 8 servings: Prepare as above, except assemble in one 9×1 1/2-inch round cake pan.

To tote: Cover tightly. Transport cake in an insulated carrier.

NUTRITION FACTS PER SERVING: 261 cal., 10 g total fat (4 g sat. fat), 17 mg chol., 282 mg sodium, 43 g carbo., 1 g fiber, 2 g pro.
DAILY VALUES: 7% vit. A, 3% vit. C, 6% calcium, 3% iron

Pineapple Cake

A coconut-pecan topping makes this pineapple cake stand out among other similar versions. The topping becomes toasty and more flavorful during baking—yum!

1 Grease a 13×9×2-inch baking pan or a 3-quart rectangular baking dish; set aside. Drain pineapple, reserving juice. Combine flour, baking powder, baking soda, and salt; set aside.

2 In a large mixing bowl beat butter with an electric mixer on medium to high speed for 30 seconds. Add granulated sugar; beat until fluffy. Add eggs; beat until smooth. Add flour mixture and reserved pineapple juice alternately to beaten mixture, beating on low speed after each addition just until combined. Fold in pineapple. Spread batter in prepared pan.

3 Combine brown sugar, pecans, and coconut; sprinkle over batter. Bake in a 350° oven for 30 to 35 minutes or until a wooden toothpick inserted in center comes out clean. Serve warm.

For 9 servings: Prepare as above, except bake in a greased 8×8×2-inch baking pan or a 2-quart square baking dish.

To tote: Cover cake tightly. Transport in an insulated carrier.

NUTRITION FACTS PER SERVING: 285 cal., 12 g total fat (5 g sat. fat), 43 mg chol., 189 mg sodium, 43 g carbo., 1 g fiber, 3 g pro.
DAILY VALUES: 5% vit. A, 6% vit. C, 5% calcium, 8% iron

PREP: 25 minutes
BAKE: 30 minutes   OVEN: 350°F

16 SERVINGS	INGREDIENTS	9 SERVINGS
1 20-oz. can	crushed pineapple	1 8-oz. can
2 1/2 cups	all-purpose flour	1 1/4 cups
1 1/2 tsp.	baking powder	3/4 tsp.
1/2 tsp.	baking soda	1/4 tsp.
1/4 tsp.	salt	1/8 tsp.
1/2 cup	butter, softened	1/4 cup
1 cup	granulated sugar	1/2 cup
2	egg(s)	1
3/4 cup	packed brown sugar	1/3 cup
3/4 cup	chopped pecans	1/3 cup
3/4 cup	coconut	1/3 cup

Oatmeal Cake

Rolled oats keep this old-fashioned cake very moist. You'll love the gooey coconut-walnut topping.

**PREP: 30 minutes BAKE: 30 minutes
STAND: 20 minutes OVEN: 350°F**

16 SERVINGS	INGREDIENTS	8 SERVINGS
1 cup	quick-cooking rolled oats	1/2 cup
1 1/2 cups	boiling water	3/4 cup
1 1/2 cups	all-purpose flour	3/4 cup
1 1/2 tsp.	ground cinnamon	3/4 tsp.
1 tsp.	baking soda	1/2 tsp.
1/2 tsp.	salt	1/4 tsp.
1/2 cup	shortening	1/4 cup
1 cup	granulated sugar	1/2 cup
1 cup	packed brown sugar	1/2 cup
2	egg(s)	1
6 Tbsp.	butter or margarine	3 Tbsp.
1 cup	flaked coconut	1/2 cup
2/3 cup	packed brown sugar	1/3 cup
2 Tbsp.	milk	1 Tbsp.
2/3 cup	chopped walnuts	1/3 cup

1 Grease a 13×9×2-inch baking pan; set pan aside. Combine oats and boiling water in a small bowl; let stand 20 minutes. Meanwhile, in a medium bowl combine flour, cinnamon, baking soda, and salt.

2 In a mixing bowl beat shortening, granulated sugar, and the 1 cup brown sugar with an electric mixer until combined. Beat in eggs. Beat in oatmeal mixture. Add flour mixture; beat until combined. Spread batter in prepared pan.

3 Bake in a 350° oven for 30 to 35 minutes or until a wooden toothpick inserted near center comes out clean. Place pan on a wire rack.

4 For topping, in a saucepan combine butter, coconut, the 2/3 cup brown sugar, and milk; cook and stir until boiling. Stir in nuts. Spoon topping over hot cake; cool completely.

For 8 servings: Prepare cake and topping as above, except spread the batter in a greased 8×8×2-inch baking pan. Bake about 25 minutes or until a wooden toothpick inserted near center comes out clean. Continue as directed.

To tote: Cover and transport in baking pan.

NUTRITION FACTS PER SERVING: 358 cal., 17 g total fat (6 g sat. fat), 39 mg chol., 218 mg sodium, 80 g carbo., 2 g fiber, 4 g pro.
DAILY VALUES: 4% vit. A, 4% calcium, 9% iron

Marble Cake

This cake will go quickly! The rich chocolate frosting is sublime. Toffee bars, although optional, make a nice contrast of crunch to the creamy frosting.

PREP: 30 minutes BAKE: 30 minutes
COOL: 2 hours OVEN: 350°F

16 SERVINGS	INGREDIENTS	9 SERVINGS
3 cups	all-purpose flour	2 cups
2¹/₂ tsp.	baking powder	1¹/₂ tsp.
³/₄ tsp.	baking soda	¹/₂ tsp.
¹/₄ tsp.	salt	¹/₄ tsp.
³/₄ cup	butter, softened	¹/₂ cup
2 cups	sugar	1¹/₃ cups
1 Tbsp.	vanilla	2 tsp.
3	eggs	2
1¹/₂ cups	milk	1 cup
¹/₂ cup	chocolate-flavored syrup	¹/₃ cup
1 recipe	Chocolate Butter Frosting	¹/₂ recipe
2 1.4-oz. bars	chocolate-covered English toffee, chopped (optional)	1 1.4-oz. bar

1 Grease a 13×9×2-inch baking pan; set pan aside. Combine flour, baking powder, baking soda, and salt; set aside.

2 In a large mixing bowl beat butter for 30 seconds. Add sugar and vanilla; beat until fluffy. Add eggs, one at a time, beating well after each. Add flour mixture and milk alternately to mixture, beating on low speed after each addition just until combined.

3 Transfer 1¹/₂ cups of batter to a medium bowl; stir in chocolate-flavored syrup. Pour light batter into the prepared pan. Spoon chocolate batter over light batter. Gently cut through batters to marble.

4 Bake in a 350° oven for 30 to 35 minutes or until a wooden toothpick comes out clean. Cool in pan on a wire rack. Frost with Chocolate Butter Frosting. If desired, sprinkle with chopped candy bars.

Chocolate Butter Frosting: In a large mixing bowl beat 6 tablespoons butter and ¹/₂ cup unsweetened cocoa powder with an electric mixer on medium speed until fluffy. Gradually add 2 cups sifted powdered sugar, beating well. Slowly beat in ¹/₄ cup milk and 1¹/₂ teaspoons vanilla. Slowly beat in an additional 2 cups sifted powdered sugar. If necessary, beat in additional milk to reach spreading consistency. Makes 2 cups.

For 9 servings: Prepare as above, except stir chocolate syrup into only 1 cup of the light batter. Pour batters into a greased 9×9×2-inch baking pan and bake for 35 to 40 minutes or until a wooden toothpick comes out clean.

NUTRITION FACTS PER SERVING: 453 cal., 16 g total fat (9 g sat. fat), 79 mg chol., 332 mg sodium, 74 g carbo., 1 g fiber, 5 g pro.
DAILY VALUES: 13% vit. A, 11% calcium, 10% iron

Pumpkin Pie Dessert

A creamy pumpkin filling crowned with a crunchy topping makes this a dessert to remember.

1 Grease a 13×9×2-inch baking pan; set aside. In a large bowl combine the pumpkin, sugar, cinnamon, salt, nutmeg, and ginger; add eggs. Beat lightly with a wooden spoon just until mixture is combined. Gradually stir in evaporated milk; mix well. Pour into prepared pan. Sprinkle dry cake mix evenly over pumpkin mixture; sprinkle evenly with nuts. Drizzle with melted butter.

2 Bake in a 350° oven about 50 minutes or until edges are firm and top is golden. Cool in pan on a wire rack. Cover and chill for at least 2 hours before serving. If desired, serve with whipped dessert topping. Store in the refrigerator.

For 9 servings: Prepare as above, except pour pumpkin mixture into a greased 8×8×2-inch baking pan and bake about 40 minutes or until edges are firm and top is golden.

To tote: Cover tightly. Transport dessert and, if desired, whipped dessert topping in an insulated cooler with ice packs.

NUTRITION FACTS PER SERVING: 328 cal., 17 g total fat (7 g sat. fat), 75 mg chol., 364 mg sodium, 41 g carbo., 2 g fiber, 5 g pro.
DAILY VALUES: 210% vit. A, 4% vit. C, 13% calcium, 9% iron

PREP: 20 minutes BAKE: 50 minutes
CHILL: 2 hours OVEN: 350°F

18 SERVINGS	INGREDIENTS	9 SERVINGS
1 29-oz. can	pumpkin	1 15-oz. can
1 cup	sugar	$1/2$ cup
1 tsp.	ground cinnamon	$1/2$ tsp.
$1/2$ tsp.	salt	$1/4$ tsp.
$1/2$ tsp.	ground nutmeg	$1/4$ tsp.
$1/2$ tsp.	ground ginger	$1/4$ tsp.
4	beaten eggs	2
1 12-oz. can ($1^1/2$ cups)	evaporated milk	1 5-oz. can ($2/3$ cup)
1 pkg. 2-layer size	yellow cake mix	1 pkg. 1-layer size
1 cup	chopped nuts	$1/2$ cup
$3/4$ cup	butter or margarine, melted	$1/3$ cup
	Frozen whipped dessert topping, thawed (optional)	

Apple Dapple Cake

Although overeating is customary at potlucks, be sure to save room for this cake. The moist cake and sauce are simply wonderful together.

PREP: 30 minutes
BAKE: 1 hour 5 minutes   OVEN: 350°F

20 SERVINGS / INGREDIENTS / 9 SERVINGS

20 SERVINGS	INGREDIENTS	9 SERVINGS
3 cups	all-purpose flour	2 cups
2 cups	granulated sugar	1¹/₃ cups
1 tsp.	baking soda	³/₄ tsp.
¹/₂ tsp.	salt	¹/₄ tsp.
3	beaten eggs	2
1 cup	cooking oil	²/₃ cup
¹/₂ cup	apple juice	¹/₃ cup
2 tsp.	vanilla	1¹/₂ tsp.
3 cups	finely chopped cooking apples	2 cups
1 cup	chopped walnuts or pecans	²/₃ cup
1 cup	packed brown sugar	²/₃ cup
¹/₄ cup	butter	3 Tbsp.
¹/₃ cup	whipping cream	¹/₄ cup

1 Grease and flour a 10-inch springform pan, or grease a 13×9×2-inch baking pan; set aside. In a very large mixing bowl combine flour, granulated sugar, baking soda, and salt; make a well in center and set aside. In a medium bowl combine eggs, oil, apple juice, and vanilla; stir in apples and nuts. Add egg mixture to flour mixture, stirring just until moistened. Spread batter in prepared pan. (Place springform pan, if using, on a baking sheet.)

2 Bake in a 350° oven about 65 minutes for springform pan or 45 to 50 minutes for 13×9-inch pan or until a toothpick inserted in center comes out clean. Cool in pan on a wire rack. (Remove sides of springform pan, if using.)

3 For sauce, in a small saucepan combine brown sugar, butter, and cream. Cook and stir over medium heat just until bubbly and all of the sugar is dissolved. Cool slightly. Drizzle warm sauce over cake.

For 9 servings: Prepare as above, except spread batter in a greased 9×9×2-inch baking pan and bake about 40 minutes or until toothpick inserted in center comes out clean.

To tote: Cover and transport in baking pan. Transport sauce in a covered container in an insulated carrier.

NUTRITION FACTS PER SERVING: 376 cal., 20 g total fat (5 g sat. fat), 44 mg chol., 162 mg sodium, 48 g carbo., 1 g fiber, 4 g pro.
DAILY VALUES: 4% vit. A, 1% vit. C, 3% calcium, 7% iron

Streusel Strawberry Bars

These bars taste like a butter cookie with strawberry filling. Strawberry or raspberry jam stands in as the filling. Sifted powdered sugar is a fine substitute for the icing if you're in a hurry.

PREP: 20 minutes BAKE: 45 minutes
COOL: 2 hours OVEN: 350°F

48 SERVINGS	INGREDIENTS	24 SERVINGS
2 cups	butter, softened	1 cup
2 cups	granulated sugar	1 cup
2	egg(s)	1
4 cups	all-purpose flour	2 cups
1 1/2 cups	pecans, coarsely chopped	3/4 cup
2 10-oz. jars	strawberry preserves or seedless red raspberry preserves	1 10-oz. jar
1 recipe	Powdered Sugar Icing or sifted powdered sugar	1 recipe

1 In a large mixing bowl beat butter and granulated sugar with an electric mixer on medium speed until combined, scraping sides of bowl occasionally. Beat in eggs. Beat in as much flour as you can with the mixer. Stir in any remaining flour and the pecans (mixture will be crumbly). Set aside 2 cups of the pecan mixture.

2 Press the remaining pecan mixture into the bottom of an ungreased 13×9×2-inch baking pan. Spread preserves to within 1/2 inch of the edges. Sprinkle reserved pecan mixture on top of preserves.

3 Bake in a 350° oven about 45 minutes or until top is golden brown. Cool in pan on a wire rack. Drizzle with Powdered Sugar Icing. Cut into bars.

Powdered Sugar Icing: In a small bowl stir together 1 cup sifted powdered sugar, 1 tablespoon milk, and 1/4 teaspoon vanilla. Stir in additional milk, 1 teaspoon at a time, until icing is of drizzling consistency.

For 24 bars: Prepare as above, except assemble and bake in a 9×9×2-inch baking pan.

NUTRITION FACTS PER BAR: 205 cal., 11 g total fat (5 g sat. fat), 31 mg chol., 89 mg sodium, 26 g carbo., 1 g fiber, 2 g pro.
DAILY VALUES: 6% vit. A, 2% vit. C, 1% calcium, 3% iron

Peach of a Crumble

Peach crumble is a perfect foil for tangy cranberries. A scoop of ginger ice cream is the crowning glory.

1 For filling, in a bowl combine granulated sugar, the 2 tablespoons flour, and cornstarch. Add peaches and cranberries; toss gently to coat. Stir in melted butter and lemon juice. Spread filling in a 2-quart square baking dish. Set aside.

2 For topping, in a small bowl combine the ³/₄ cup flour, brown sugar, baking powder, baking soda, and salt. Cut in the cold butter until mixture resembles coarse crumbs. Sprinkle topping and almonds over filling.

3 Bake in a 375° oven about 40 minutes or until filling is bubbly and topping is golden. Serve warm.

For 4 servings: Prepare as above, except spread filling in a 1-quart casserole and bake about 50 minutes* or until filling is bubbly and topping is golden.

To tote: Cover dish tightly. Transport in an insulated carrier.

*NOTE: Due to the thicker amount of topping in a smaller dish, the timing is slightly more than the larger version.

NUTRITION FACTS PER SERVING: 307 cal., 13 g total fat (7 g sat. fat), 29 mg chol., 203 mg sodium, 47 g carbo., 4 g fiber, 3 g pro.
DAILY VALUES: 20% vit. A, 18% vit. C, 4% calcium, 7% iron

PREP: 30 minutes
BAKE: 40 minutes   OVEN: 375°F

8 SERVINGS	INGREDIENTS	4 SERVINGS
¹/₃ cup	granulated sugar	3 Tbsp.
2 Tbsp.	all-purpose flour	1 Tbsp.
1 Tbsp.	cornstarch	1¹/₂ tsp.
5 cups	sliced, peeled peaches or frozen unsweetened peach slices, thawed (do not drain)	2¹/₂ cups
1¹/₂ cups	cranberries	³/₄ cup
¹/₄ cup	butter, melted	2 Tbsp.
1 Tbsp.	lemon juice	1¹/₂ tsp.
³/₄ cup	all-purpose flour	¹/₃ cup
¹/₂ cup	packed brown sugar	¹/₄ cup
¹/₄ tsp.	baking powder	¹/₈ tsp.
¹/₄ tsp.	baking soda	¹/₈ tsp.
¹/₈ tsp.	salt	Dash
3 Tbsp.	cold butter	4¹/₂ tsp.
¹/₄ cup	sliced almonds	2 Tbsp.

Tiramisù

This classic Italian dessert is great for two reasons: It can be made up to 24 hours in advance and it tastes so good you won't have to worry about toting home leftovers.

PREP: 30 minutes   CHILL: 4 to 24 hours

15 SERVINGS — INGREDIENTS — 8 SERVINGS

15 SERVINGS	INGREDIENTS	8 SERVINGS
1/2 cup	strong coffee	1/4 cup
2 Tbsp.	coffee liqueur	1 Tbsp.
2 8-oz. cartons	dairy sour cream	1 8-oz. carton
2 8-oz. pkgs.	cream cheese, softened	1 8-oz. pkg.
2/3 cup	sugar	1/3 cup
1/4 cup	milk	2 Tbsp.
1/2 tsp.	vanilla	1/4 tsp.
2 3-oz. pkgs.	ladyfingers, split	1 3-oz. pkg.
2 Tbsp.	unsweetened cocoa powder	1 Tbsp.

1 Combine coffee and coffee liqueur; set aside. In a large mixing bowl combine sour cream, cream cheese, sugar, milk, and vanilla. Beat with an electric mixer on high speed until smooth.

2 Layer one package of the ladyfingers, cut side up, in a 2-quart rectangular baking dish; brush with half of the coffee mixture. Spread with half of the cream cheese mixture. Repeat with remaining ladyfingers, coffee mixture, and cream cheese mixture. Sift cocoa powder over the top. Cover and chill for 4 to 24 hours. To serve, cut into squares.

For 8 servings: Prepare as above, except assemble in a 9×5×3-inch loaf pan lined with plastic wrap. To serve, lift from pan to a cutting board using the plastic wrap. Slice to serve.

To tote: Cover tightly. Transport in an insulated cooler with ice packs.

NUTRITION FACTS PER SERVING: 248 cal., 18 g total fat (11 g sat. fat), 66 mg chol., 134 mg sodium, 18 g carbo., 0 g fiber, 4 g pro.
DAILY VALUES: 14% vit. A, 8% calcium, 4% iron

Praline Cheesecake Squares

As with most cheesecakes, this one is very rich and should be cut into small servings. Cheesecakes are best when served the next day. So take advantage of this built-in bonus.

PREP: 40 minutes BAKE: 50 minutes
CHILL: 2 to 24 hours OVEN: 350°F

48 SERVINGS	INGREDIENTS	24 SERVINGS
2¹/₂ cups	all-purpose flour	1¹/₄ cups
1 cup	butter, melted	¹/₂ cup
²/₃ cup	finely chopped pecans	¹/₃ cup
2 Tbsp.	powdered sugar	1 Tbsp.
3 8-oz. pkgs.	cream cheese, softened	12 oz.
4	eggs	2
1 14-oz. can	sweetened condensed milk	²/₃ cup
²/₃ cup	granulated sugar	¹/₃ cup
2 tsp.	vanilla	1 tsp.
1 cup	packed brown sugar	¹/₂ cup
1 cup	whipping cream	¹/₂ cup
1 cup	chopped pecans	¹/₂ cup
1¹/₂ tsp.	vanilla	1 tsp.

1 For crust, in a large bowl combine flour, melted butter, the ²/₃ cup finely chopped pecans, and the powdered sugar; mix well. Press mixture into the bottom of a 13×9×2-inch baking pan. Bake in a 350° oven for 15 to 20 minutes or until crust is set and light golden brown around the edges.

2 Meanwhile, for filling, in a large mixing bowl beat cream cheese with an electric mixer on low to medium speed until smooth. Add eggs; beat well. Beat in sweetened condensed milk, granulated sugar, and the 2 teaspoons vanilla. Pour filling over baked crust. Bake in a 350° oven for 35 to 40 minutes until set. Cool in pan on a wire rack.

3 For topping, in a medium saucepan combine brown sugar and whipping cream. Cook and stir over medium heat until mixture boils; reduce heat. Simmer, uncovered, for 10 minutes. Remove from heat. Stir in the 1 cup chopped pecans and the 1¹/₂ teaspoons vanilla. Pour topping over cheesecake. Cover and chill for 2 to 24 hours before serving. Cut into squares.

For 24 servings: Prepare as above, except assemble and bake in an 8×8×2-inch baking pan.

To tote: Cover tightly. Transport in an insulated cooler with ice packs. (Or cut into squares and place in a single layer in a shallow container. Cover and transport in an insulated cooler with ice packs.)

NUTRITION FACTS PER SQUARE: 214 cal., 15 g total fat (8 g sat. fat), 54 mg chol., 103 mg sodium, 18 g carbo., 1 g fiber, 3 g pro.
DAILY VALUES: 10% vit. A, 5% calcium, 4% iron

Strawberry Delight

This best-loved dessert is not too sweet, as some fresh strawberry pies can be. When they are in season, substitute fresh peaches or nectarines for strawberries and use peach-flavored gelatin instead of strawberry gelatin.

1 For crust, combine the 1½ cups flour and the melted butter; stir in pecans. Pat evenly in the bottom of a 3-quart rectangular baking dish. Bake in a 350° oven about 20 minutes or until golden brown around edges. Cool in pan on a wire rack.

2 In a large mixing bowl beat powdered sugar and cream cheese with an electric mixer on medium speed until combined. Add whipped topping by spoonfuls; beat until smooth. Spread over cooled crust. Arrange sliced strawberries on top. Cover and chill while preparing top layer.

3 For top layer, in a medium saucepan combine granulated sugar, the ¼ cup flour, and the strawberry-flavored gelatin; stir in water. Cook and stir until thickened and bubbly. Cook and stir 1 minute more. Remove from heat. Cover surface and set aside to cool (about 30 minutes).

4 Spoon cooled gelatin mixture over strawberries. Cover and chill for 4 to 24 hours. Cut into squares.

For 8 servings: Prepare as above, except press the crust mixture into a 2-quart square baking dish.

To tote: Transport dessert in an insulated cooler with ice packs.

NUTRITION FACTS PER SERVING: 389 cal., 22 g total fat (12 g sat. fat), 43 mg chol., 152 mg sodium, 46 g carbo., 2 g fiber, 4 g pro.
DAILY VALUES: 12% vit. A, 27% vit. C, 3% calcium, 6% iron

PREP: 30 minutes BAKE: 20 minutes COOL: 30 minutes
CHILL: 4 to 24 hours OVEN: 350°F

15 SERVINGS | INGREDIENTS | 8 SERVINGS

15 SERVINGS	INGREDIENTS	8 SERVINGS
1½ cups	all-purpose flour	¾ cup
¾ cup	butter, melted	⅓ cup
¾ cup	chopped pecans	⅓ cup
2 cups	sifted powdered sugar	1 cup
1 8-oz. pkg.	cream cheese, softened	½ 8-oz. pkg.
1 8-oz. carton	frozen whipped dessert topping, thawed	½ 8-oz. carton
3 cups	sliced strawberries	1½ cups
1 cup	granulated sugar	½ cup
¼ cup	all-purpose flour	2 Tbsp.
3 Tbsp.	strawberry-flavored gelatin	4½ tsp.
1 cup	water	½ cup

Mini Almond Cheesecakes

These almond-crusted treats can be made well in advance and frozen individually. Sprinkle each bite-size dessert with a few slivered almonds.

1 Grease twenty-four 1³/₄-inch muffin cups. Sprinkle about 1 teaspoon of the ground almonds into each cup. Gently shake so that almonds coat bottoms and sides of cups (do not shake out excess nuts). Set aside.

2 For filling, in a medium mixing bowl combine cream cheese and granulated sugar. Beat with an electric mixer on medium speed until smooth. Add egg, the ¹/₂ teaspoon vanilla, and almond extract. Beat just until combined. Spoon filling into prepared muffin cups, filling each three-fourths full.

3 Bake in a 350° oven about 18 minutes or until tops just begin to turn golden. Cool in pans on a wire rack. Using a table knife, carefully loosen sides of cheesecakes from edges of cups. Carefully lift out of cups using the knife.

4 For topping, in a small bowl stir together the sour cream, powdered sugar, and the ¹/₄ teaspoon vanilla. Spread topping on cooled cheesecakes. Cover; chill up to 6 hours. Before serving, garnish each cheesecake with a few slivered almonds.

For 12 cheesecakes: Prepare as above, except prepare only 12 muffin cups.

Make-ahead directions: Freeze cheesecakes (without sour cream topping) in a single layer in a freezer container for up to 2 months. Thaw in the refrigerator overnight. Prepare and spread on the topping just before serving.

To tote: Place cheesecakes in a single layer in a covered container. Transport in an insulated cooler with ice packs.

NUTRITION FACTS PER CHEESECAKE: 84 cal., 6 g total fat (3 g sat. fat), 20 mg chol., 32 mg sodium, 6 g carbo., 0 g fiber, 2 g pro.
DAILY VALUES: 3% vit. A, 2% calcium, 2% iron

PREP: 25 minutes BAKE: 18 minutes
CHILL: Up to 6 hours OVEN: 350°F

24 SERVINGS	INGREDIENTS	12 SERVINGS
¹/₂ cup	slivered almonds, toasted and ground	¹/₄ cup
1 8-oz. pkg.	cream cheese, softened	¹/₂ 8-oz. pkg.
¹/₂ cup	granulated sugar	¹/₄ cup
1	egg	1
¹/₂ tsp.	vanilla	¹/₄ tsp.
¹/₂ tsp.	almond extract	¹/₄ tsp.
¹/₃ cup	dairy sour cream	3 Tbsp.
2 Tbsp.	powdered sugar	1 Tbsp.
¹/₄ tsp.	vanilla	Few drops

Biscuit Bread Pudding with Lemon Sauce

If you don't have homemade biscuits to use in this bread pudding, don't worry. You can use the refrigerated variety.

PREP: 30 minutes   STAND: 10 minutes
BAKE: 45 minutes   OVEN: 350°F

12 SERVINGS	INGREDIENTS	8 SERVINGS
6	slightly beaten eggs	4
1 12-oz. can plus 1 5-oz. can	evaporated milk	1 12-oz. can
2¹/₂ cups	sugar	1³/₄ cups
¹/₃ cup	butter or margarine, melted	¹/₄ cup
1¹/₂ tsp.	vanilla	1 tsp.
³/₄ tsp.	ground cinnamon	¹/₂ tsp.
³/₄ tsp.	ground nutmeg	¹/₂ tsp.
9 cups (12 to 15 biscuits)	coarsely crumbled buttermilk biscuits*	6 cups (8 to 10 biscuits)
1 recipe	Lemon Sauce	¹/₂ recipe

1 In a large bowl stir together eggs, evaporated milk, sugar, melted butter, vanilla, cinnamon, and nutmeg. Place crumbled biscuits in a greased 3-quart rectangular baking dish. Pour egg mixture over biscuits, pressing to moisten evenly. Let stand for 10 minutes to thoroughly moisten biscuits.

2 Bake in a 350° oven about 45 minutes or until a knife inserted near center comes out clean. Serve warm with Lemon Sauce.

Lemon Sauce: In a medium saucepan stir together 2 beaten eggs, ¹/₄ cup water, and ¹/₄ cup lemon juice. Add 1 cup sugar and ¹/₂ cup butter, cut up. Cook and stir until mixture is thickened and just bubbly on edges. If desired, strain sauce. Serve warm. Store in the refrigerator. Makes about 2 cups.

For 8 servings: Omit the 5-ounce can evaporated milk. Prepare as above, except place biscuits in a 2-quart square baking dish. Bake about 35 minutes or until knife inserted in center comes out clean.

To tote: Cover tightly. Transport in an insulated carrier. Transport sauce in a covered container in an insulated carrier.

*NOTE: Use homemade biscuits or 2 packages refrigerated large Southern-style biscuits, baked according to package directions.

NUTRITION FACTS PER SERVING: 577 cal., 26 g total fat (13 g sat. fat), 190 mg chol., 702 mg sodium, 80 g carbo., 0 g fiber, 10 g pro.
DAILY VALUES: 16% vit. A, 5% vit. C, 13% calcium, 9% iron

Fudgy Brownies

These luscious brownies have a mild coffee flavor. If you're not a coffee fan, omit the coffee crystals.

1 Line a 13×9×2-inch baking pan with foil, extending foil over edges of pan. Grease foil; set pan aside.

2 In a large microwave-safe mixing bowl combine the chocolate, butter, water, and coffee crystals. Microwave, uncovered, on 100% power (high) for 2 to 4 minutes or until butter is melted, stirring once or twice. Remove bowl from microwave oven. Stir until chocolate is completely melted.

3 Beat in granulated sugar and brown sugar with an electric mixer on low to medium speed until combined. Add eggs and vanilla; beat on medium speed for 2 minutes. Add flour, almonds, cinnamon, and salt. Beat on low speed until combined. Spread batter in prepared pan.

4 Bake in a 350° oven about 35 minutes or until top appears set and dry. Cool in pan on a wire rack. Use foil to lift brownies out of pan. Cut into bars. If desired, stir together the powdered sugar and cocoa powder; sift over brownies.

For 16 brownies: Prepare as above, except spread batter in a greased and foil-lined 9×9×2-inch baking pan.

To tote: Cover and transport in baking pan. (Or cut into bars and place in a single layer in a shallow container.)

NUTRITION FACTS PER BROWNIE: 302 cal., 17 g total fat (9 g sat. fat), 66 mg chol., 127 mg sodium, 37 g carbo., 2 g fiber, 4 g pro.
DAILY VALUES: 8% vit. A, 4% calcium, 10% iron

PREP: 15 minutes
BAKE: 35 minutes   OVEN: 350°F

24 SERVINGS	INGREDIENTS	16 SERVINGS
9 oz.	unsweetened chocolate, coarsely chopped	6 ounces
1 cup	butter	3/4 cup
1/3 cup	water	1/4 cup
4 tsp.	instant coffee crystals	1 Tbsp.
1 1/2 cups	granulated sugar	1 cup
1 1/2 cups	packed brown sugar	1 cup
5	eggs	3
1 1/2 tsp.	vanilla	1 tsp.
2 cups	all-purpose flour	1 1/4 cups
3/4 cup	ground almonds	1/2 cup
1/2 tsp.	ground cinnamon	1/4 tsp.
1/4 tsp.	salt	1/8 tsp.
3 Tbsp.	powdered sugar (optional)	2 Tbsp.
1/4 tsp.	unsweetened cocoa powder (optional)	1/4 tsp.

Almond Squares

These squares taste like toasted almond—the secret is in the topping. Yet another recipe you'd better be prepared to share!

PREP: 25 minutes BAKE: 20 minutes
BROIL: 1 minute OVEN: 350°F

32 SERVINGS	INGREDIENTS	16 SERVINGS
2	egg(s)	1
1 cup	sugar	1/2 cup
1 cup	butter, melted	1/2 cup
1 cup	all-purpose flour	1/2 cup
1/2 cup	butter	1/4 cup
1/2 cup	sugar	1/4 cup
1/2 cup	sliced almonds	1/4 cup
1 Tbsp.	all-purpose flour	1 1/2 tsp.
1 Tbsp.	milk	1 1/2 tsp.

1 Grease and lightly flour a 13×9×2-inch baking pan; set pan aside.

2 For crust, in a medium mixing bowl beat eggs and the 1 cup sugar with an electric mixer on medium speed about 8 minutes or until thick and lemon-colored. Stir in the 1 cup melted butter and the 1 cup flour. Pour into prepared pan.

3 Bake in a 350° oven for 20 to 25 minutes or until a wooden toothpick inserted near center comes out clean and edges begin to pull away from pan.

4 Meanwhile, for topping, in small saucepan combine the 1/2 cup butter, the 1/2 cup sugar, the almonds, the 1 tablespoon flour, and the milk. Cook and stir over medium heat until mixture comes to a boil.

5 Adjust oven rack so top of pan is 3 to 4 inches from heat. Spoon almond mixture over hot crust. Broil about 1 minute or until golden, watching carefully to avoid burning. Cool in pan on a wire rack. Cut into bars.

For 16 bars: Prepare as above, except assemble and bake in an 8×8×2-inch baking pan.

To tote: Cover and transport squares in baking pan. (Or cut into bars and place in a single layer in a shallow container.)

NUTRITION FACTS PER BAR: 147 cal., 11 g total fat (6 g sat. fat), 38 mg chol., 97 mg sodium, 12 g carbo., 0 g fiber, 1 g pro.
DAILY VALUES: 7% vit. A, 1% calcium, 2% iron

Espresso Brownies

Because this fudgy brownie isn't cloyingly sweet, you'll definitely notice the intense coffee and chocolate flavors.

1 Line a 13×9×2-inch baking pan with foil, extending foil over edges of pan. Grease foil; set pan aside. Melt butter and unsweetened chocolate in a small saucepan over low heat, stirring constantly. Cool mixture to room temperature.

2 Meanwhile, in a medium bowl stir together flour, baking powder, and salt; set aside. In a large mixing bowl beat eggs, sugar, espresso powder, coffee liqueur, and vanilla with an electric mixer until combined. Beat in cooled chocolate mixture. Add flour mixture, stirring just until combined. Spread batter evenly in prepared pan.

3 Bake in a 350° oven for 25 to 30 minutes until top appears set and dry. Cool in pan on a wire rack. Pour Chocolate Glaze evenly over brownies. Cover and chill about 2 hours until glaze is set.

4 Before serving, let stand at room temperature for 20 to 30 minutes. Use foil to lift brownies out of pan. Cut into bars. If desired, garnish with chocolate-covered coffee beans.

Chocolate Glaze: In a medium saucepan combine 6 ounces coarsely chopped semisweet chocolate, 1/4 cup butter, and 2 tablespoons milk. Cook and stir over low heat until melted and smooth.

For 24 brownies: Prepare as above, except spread the batter in a greased and foil-lined 8×8×2-inch baking pan.

To tote: Cover and transport in baking pan. (Or cut into bars and place in a single layer in a shallow container.)

NUTRITION FACTS PER BAR: 144 cal., 9 g total fat (5 g sat. fat), 31 mg chol., 91 mg sodium, 16 g carbo., 1 g fiber, 2 g pro.
DAILY VALUES: 4% vit. A, 1% calcium, 4% iron

PREP: 25 minutes BAKE: 25 minutes
CHILL: 2 hours OVEN: 350°F

48 SERVINGS	INGREDIENTS	24 SERVINGS
1 cup	butter, cut into pieces	1/2 cup
6 oz.	unsweetened chocolate, coarsely chopped	3 oz.
1 1/2 cups	all-purpose flour	3/4 cup
1 tsp.	baking powder	1/2 tsp.
1/2 tsp.	salt	1/4 tsp.
4	eggs	2
2 1/2 cups	sugar	1 1/4 cups
1/4 cup	instant espresso powder	2 Tbsp.
1/4 cup	coffee-flavored liqueur	2 Tbsp.
2 tsp.	vanilla	1 tsp.
1 recipe	Chocolate Glaze	1/2 recipe
	Chocolate-covered coffee beans (optional)	

Carrot Cake

Like any carrot cake, the cream cheese frosting is a must. What a great way to eat your vegetables!

PREP: 20 minutes BAKE: 40 minutes
COOL: 2 hours OVEN: 350°F

16 SERVINGS	INGREDIENTS	12 SERVINGS
2 cups	all-purpose flour	1 cup
2 cups	sugar	1 cup
2 tsp.	baking powder	1 tsp.
1 tsp.	ground cinnamon	1/2 tsp.
1/2 tsp.	baking soda	1/4 tsp.
3 cups	finely shredded carrots	1 1/2 cups
1 cup	cooking oil	1/2 cup
4	eggs	2
1 cup	chopped pecans	1/2 cup
1 recipe	Cream Cheese Frosting	1/2 recipe

1 Grease a 13×9×2-inch baking pan; set pan aside. In a large mixing bowl stir together the flour, sugar, baking powder, cinnamon, and baking soda. Add finely shredded carrots, cooking oil, and eggs. Beat with an electric mixer just until combined. Stir in chopped pecans. Spread batter in prepared pan.

2 Bake in a 350° oven for 40 to 45 minutes or until a wooden toothpick comes out clean. Cool in pan on a wire rack. Frost with Cream Cheese Frosting. Cover and store in the refrigerator.

Cream Cheese Frosting: In a medium mixing bowl beat together 6 ounces cream cheese, softened, and 2 teaspoons vanilla with an electric mixer until light and fluffy. Gradually add 2 cups sifted powdered sugar, beating well. Gradually beat in 2 to 2 1/2 cups additional sifted powdered sugar to reach spreading consistency. Makes about 1 1/2 cups frosting.

For 12 servings: Prepare as above, except spread batter in a greased 8×8×2-inch baking pan and bake about 30 minutes or until a wooden toothpick comes out clean.

To tote: Transport cake in an insulated cooler with ice packs.

NUTRITION FACTS PER SERVING: 481 cal., 24 g total fat (5 g sat. fat), 65 mg chol., 145 mg sodium, 65 g carbo., 2 g fiber, 5 g pro.
DAILY VALUES: 121% vit. A, 4% vit. C, 7% calcium, 9% iron

Chocolate Goody Bars

A fudge brownie mix shaves some prep time in the kitchen. The peanutty crunchy topping is spread over purchased vanilla frosting.

PREP: 20 minutes BAKE: 30 minutes
CHILL: 1¹/₂ hours OVEN: 350°F

36 SERVINGS / INGREDIENTS / 16 SERVINGS

36 SERVINGS	INGREDIENTS	16 SERVINGS
1 19.8-oz. pkg.	fudge brownie mix	1 8-oz. pkg.
¹/₂ cup	cooking oil	1 Tbsp.
2	egg(s)	1
¹/₄ cup	water	1 Tbsp.
1 16-oz. can	vanilla frosting	¹/₃ 16-oz. can (¹/₂ cup)
³/₄ cup	chopped peanuts	¹/₄ cup
1 12-oz. pkg.	semisweet chocolate pieces	²/₃ cup
1 cup	creamy peanut butter	¹/₃ cup
3 cups	crisp rice cereal	1 cup

1 Line a 13×9×2-inch baking pan with foil, extending foil over edges of the pan. Grease foil; set pan aside.

2 In a large bowl stir together the brownie mix, oil, eggs, and water. Spread batter in prepared pan. Bake in a 350° oven for 30 minutes. Cool completely on a wire rack.

3 Frost bars with vanilla frosting. Sprinkle with peanuts. Cover and chill about 45 minutes or until frosting is firm.

4 Meanwhile, in a medium saucepan combine chocolate pieces and peanut butter. Cook and stir over low heat until chocolate is melted; stir in cereal. Spread over frosting, Cover and chill about 45 minutes more or until chocolate layer is set. Use foil to lift out of pan. Cut into bars. Store in the refrigerator.

For 16 bars: Prepare as above, except assemble in a greased and foil-lined 9×5×3 inch loaf pan and bake for 25 minutes.

To tote: Cover and transport in baking pan in an insulated cooler with ice packs. (Or cut into bars and place in a single layer in a shallow container. Transport in an insulated cooler with ice packs.)

NUTRITION FACTS PER SERVING: 264 cal., 14 g total fat (4 g sat. fat), 12 mg chol., 140 mg sodium, 28 g carbo., 2 g fiber, 4 g pro.
DAILY VALUES: 2% vit. A, 2% vit. C, 1% calcium, 6% iron

Blueberry Crisp

There is no better way to utilize blueberries in the summer months than with blueberry crisp. A scoop of vanilla ice cream adds to the dessert's perfection.

PREP: 20 minutes
BAKE: 30 minutes   OVEN: 375°F

INGREDIENTS

8 SERVINGS		4 SERVINGS
3 Tbsp.	all-purpose flour	4 tsp.
2 Tbsp.	granulated sugar	1 Tbsp.
6 cups	blueberries	3 cups
1/4 cup	lemon juice	2 Tbsp.
1 cup	packed brown sugar	2/3 cup
3/4 cup	all-purpose flour	1/2 cup
3/4 cup	quick-cooking rolled oats	1/2 cup
1 1/4 tsp.	ground cinnamon	3/4 tsp.
1/2 cup	cold butter	1/3 cup

1 In a large bowl stir together the 3 tablespoons flour and granulated sugar. Add blueberries and lemon juice; toss gently to combine. Spread berry mixture evenly in a 3-quart rectangular baking dish; set aside.

2 For topping, combine brown sugar, the 3/4 cup flour, oats, and cinnamon. Using a pastry blender, cut in butter until mixture resembles coarse crumbs. Sprinkle topping evenly over berries.

3 Bake in a 375° oven about 30 minutes or until topping is golden brown and edges are bubbly. Serve warm.

For 4 servings: Prepare as above, except assemble and bake in a 2-quart square baking dish.

To tote: Cover tightly. Transport crisp in an insulated carrier.

NUTRITION FACTS PER SERVING: 371 cal., 13 g total fat (8 g sat. fat), 33 mg chol., 142 mg sodium, 63 g carbo., 4 g fiber, 4 g pro.
DAILY VALUES: 11% vit. A, 29% vit. C, 5% calcium, 10% iron

Cranberry-Apple Casserole

This fruit casserole is really like a cobbler. Instead of measuring oatmeal for the topping, open a package of instant oatmeal. It has all of the spices already added.

1 In a large bowl stir together the granulated sugar and the 2 tablespoons flour. Add apple slices and cranberries; toss to coat. Transfer the fruit mixture to a 2-quart casserole.

2 For topping, in a medium bowl combine oatmeal, pecans, brown sugar, and the ¹/₃ cup flour. Stir in butter until moistened. Spoon evenly over fruit. Bake in a 350° oven about 45 minutes or until fruit is tender. If necessary to prevent overbrowning, cover loosely with foil for the last 10 minutes of baking. Serve warm.

For 4 servings: Prepare as above, except assemble and bake in a 1-quart casserole.

To tote: Cover casserole dish tightly. Transport in an insulated carrier.

NUTRITION FACTS PER SERVING: 372 cal., 16 g total fat (6 g sat. fat), 22 mg chol., 148 mg sodium, 58 g carbo., 4 g fiber, 3 g pro.
DAILY VALUES: 12% vit. A, 11% vit. C, 5% calcium, 11% iron

PREP: 20 minutes
BAKE: 45 minutes OVEN: 350°F

8 SERVINGS	INGREDIENTS	4 SERVINGS
²/₃ cup	granulated sugar	¹/₃ cup
2 Tbsp.	all-purpose flour	1 Tbsp.
4 cups	sliced, peeled apples	2 cups
2 cups	cranberries	1 cup
2 1.23-oz. envelopes	instant oatmeal with cinnamon and spice	1 1.23-oz. envelope
³/₄ cup	chopped pecans	¹/₃ cup
¹/₂ cup	packed brown sugar	¹/₄ cup
¹/₃ cup	all-purpose flour	3 Tbsp.
¹/₃ cup	butter, melted	3 Tbsp.

Candy Bar Cookies

Is it a cookie or candy? You decide. Either way, this treat is always a hit at potlucks and family gatherings.

1 Line a 13×9×2-inch baking pan with foil, extending foil over edges of pan; set pan aside. In a medium saucepan cook and stir brown sugar, butter, and corn syrup over medium-low heat until combined. Remove saucepan from heat; stir in the ¼ cup peanut butter and the vanilla until smooth.

2 For crust, place rolled oats in a very large bowl. Pour brown sugar mixture over oats, stirring gently until combined. Press oat mixture evenly onto bottom of prepared baking pan. Bake in a 375° oven for 10 to 12 minutes or until edges are light brown.

3 Meanwhile, in the same medium saucepan cook and stir chocolate pieces and butterscotch pieces together over low heat until melted. Stir in the ⅔ cup peanut butter until mixture is smooth. Slowly pour mixture over the hot crust, spreading evenly; sprinkle with peanuts.

4 Cool in pan on a wire rack for several hours or until chocolate layer is firm. (If necessary, chill until chocolate is set.) When firm, use foil to lift out of pan. Cut into bars.

For 32 bars: Prepare as above, except press crust into a foil-lined 8×8×2-inch baking pan.

To tote: Cover and transport cookies in baking pan. (Or cut into bars and place in a single layer in a shallow container.)

NUTRITION FACTS PER BAR: 166 cal., 9 g total fat (4 g sat. fat), 7 mg chol., 64 mg sodium, 16 g carbo., 2 g fiber, 3 g pro.
DAILY VALUES: 2% vit. A, 1% calcium, 3% iron

PREP: 30 minutes
BAKE: 10 minutes   OVEN: 375°F

48 SERVINGS	INGREDIENTS	32 SERVINGS
1 cup	packed brown sugar	½ cup
⅔ cup	butter or margarine	⅓ cup
¼ cup	dark- or light-colored corn syrup	2 Tbsp.
¼ cup	peanut butter	2 Tbsp.
1 tsp.	vanilla	½ tsp.
3½ cups	quick-cooking rolled oats	1¾ cups
2 cups	semisweet chocolate pieces	1 cup
1 cup	butterscotch pieces	½ cup
⅔ cup	peanut butter	⅓ cup
½ cup	chopped peanuts	¼ cup

INDEX

Metric Information

The charts on this page provide a guide for converting measurements from the U.S. customary system, which is used throughout this book, to the metric system.

Product Differences

Most of the ingredients called for in the recipes in this book are available in most countries. However, some are known by different names. Here are some common American ingredients and their possible counterparts:

- Sugar (white) is granulated, fine granulated, or castor sugar.
- Powdered sugar is icing sugar.
- All-purpose flour is enriched, bleached or unbleached white household flour. When self-rising flour is used in place of all-purpose flour in a recipe that calls for leavening, omit the leavening agent (baking soda or baking powder) and salt.
- Light-colored corn syrup is golden syrup.
- Cornstarch is cornflour.
- Baking soda is bicarbonate of soda.
- Vanilla or vanilla extract is vanilla essence.
- Green, red, or yellow sweet peppers are capsicums or bell peppers.
- Golden raisins are sultanas.

Volume and Weight

The United States traditionally uses cup measures for liquid and solid ingredients. The chart below shows the approximate imperial and metric equivalents. If you are accustomed to weighing solid ingredients, the following approximate equivalents will be helpful.

- 1 cup butter, castor sugar, or rice = 8 ounces = 1/2 pound = 250 grams
- 1 cup flour = 4 ounces = 1/4 pound = 125 grams
- 1 cup icing sugar = 5 ounces = 150 grams

Canadian and U.S. volume for a cup measure is 8 fluid ounces (237 ml), but the standard metric equivalent is 250 ml.

1 British imperial cup is 10 fluid ounces.

In Australia, 1 tablespoon equals 20 ml, and there are 4 teaspoons in the Australian tablespoon.

Spoon measures are used for smaller amounts of ingredients. Although the size of the tablespoon varies slightly in different countries, for practical purposes and for recipes in this book, a straight substitution is all that's necessary. Measurements made using cups or spoons always should be level unless stated otherwise.

Common Weight Range Replacements

Imperial / U.S.	Metric
1/2 ounce	15 g
1 ounce	25 g or 30 g
4 ounces (1/4 pound)	115 g or 125 g
8 ounces (1/2 pound)	225 g or 250 g
16 ounces (1 pound)	450 g or 500 g
1 1/4 pounds	625 g
1 1/2 pounds	750 g
2 pounds or 2 1/4 pounds	1,000 g or 1 Kg

Oven Temperature Equivalents

Fahrenheit Setting	Celsius Setting*	Gas Setting
300°F	150°C	Gas Mark 2 (very low)
325°F	160°C	Gas Mark 3 (low)
350°F	180°C	Gas Mark 4 (moderate)
375°F	190°C	Gas Mark 5 (moderate)
400°F	200°C	Gas Mark 6 (hot)
425°F	220°C	Gas Mark 7 (hot)
450°F	230°C	Gas Mark 8 (very hot)
475°F	240°C	Gas Mark 9 (very hot)
500°F	260°C	Gas Mark 10 (extremely hot)
Broil	Broil	Grill

*Electric and gas ovens may be calibrated using celsius. However, for an electric oven, increase celsius setting 10 to 20 degrees when cooking above 160°C. For convection or forced air ovens (gas or electric) lower the temperature setting 25°F/10°C when cooking at all heat levels.

Baking Pan Sizes

Imperial / U.S.	Metric
9×1 1/2-inch round cake pan	22- or 23×4-cm (1.5 L)
9×1 1/2-inch pie plate	22- or 23×4-cm (1 L)
8×8×2-inch square cake pan	20×5-cm (2 L)
9×9×2-inch square cake pan	22- or 23×4.5-cm (2.5 L)
11×7×1 1/2-inch baking pan	28×17×4-cm (2 L)
2-quart rectangular baking pan	30×19×4.5-cm (3 L)
13×9×2-inch baking pan	34×22×4.5-cm (3.5 L)
15×10×1-inch jelly roll pan	40×25×2-cm
9×5×3-inch loaf pan	23×13×8-cm (2 L)
2-quart casserole	2 L

U.S. / Standard Metric Equivalents

1/8 teaspoon = 0.5 ml	
1/4 teaspoon = 1 ml	
1/2 teaspoon = 2 ml	
1 teaspoon = 5 ml	
1 tablespoon = 15 ml	
2 tablespoons = 25 ml	
1/4 cup = 2 fluid ounces = 50 ml	
1/3 cup = 3 fluid ounces = 75 ml	
1/2 cup = 4 fluid ounces = 125 ml	
2/3 cup = 5 fluid ounces = 150 ml	
3/4 cup = 6 fluid ounces = 175 ml	
1 cup = 8 fluid ounces = 250 ml	
2 cups = 1 pint = 500 ml	
1 quart = 1 litre	